The Happy Millionaire

*An Effortless Technique
to Achieve, Manage, and Enjoy Wealth*

By Jacob Korthuis

The Happy Millionaire – An Effortless Technique to Achieve, Manage and Enjoy Wealth

© Copyright 2008 First English edition

ISBN: 0-9786598-5-6
ISBN EAN13:   978-0-9786598-5-1
Publisher: PMA Institute
               PO Box 470475
               Celebration, FL 34747
               USA

www.pmainstitute.com
(Main Office and Training Institute)

Content

About the writer

Jacob Korthuis was born in the Netherlands in 1950. He lived there until 2002, then moved to Florida.

From 1979 to 2002, he practiced holistic health and became the personal coach for many executives in the corporate field. He also wrote several books related to health and happiness. In 1991, he appeared on national television in the Netherlands, where he represented the Dutch professional holistic health community.

In 1996, he developed an entirely new approach to solving psychological and psychosomatic complaints, as well as behavioral problems. This method, called *Progressive Mental Alignment®* (PMA), helps people transform their unhealthy, inhibiting, and sabotaging belief systems into empowering, motivating, and proactive behavior. Korthuis has since trained hundreds of professionals in the healthcare business and in the corporate world on how to apply the PMA technique to their own lives and become healthy, wealthy, and happy.

Preface

More than ever, people all over the world are looking for guidance – for answers to their questions about health, relationships, communication, beliefs, and prosperity. As the developer of the *Progressive Mental Alignment*® (*PMA*) *Technique*, I've written books that provide scientific explanations about how our brain works and how we can change those things and behaviors that we don't like. Generally, people who are interested in real growth in every aspect of their lives, are mainly interested in valuable, new, information that will explain the how to's of a new method like this. That, dear readers, is the basis of this book.

At some point at the beginning of my writing, I realized that the majority of people who look for answers and direction are not very interested in *why* something works but are, in fact, a lot more interested in *what they have to do* to make that something work. For instance, when I suffered from a headache, I wanted it to stop. I wasn't interested in the name of the medicine, its origin or what the ingredients or scientific facts were. The only thing I wanted to know was: *Where can I buy that medicine, how do I have to take it, and how fast will it get rid of my headache?*

Nevertheless, when an approach is new to us, we all need some explanation about it before we venture to use it. So, I decided to write a book that provides this information about *the PMA belief system transformation technique* and, more importantly, directions on how to use this technique successfully. This book will give you information about a straightforward technique that's unbelievably effective and powerful from the very first moment you apply it. Although there are many facets to *PMA* application, in this book, I have restricted that application to one subject: *How to become and remain a happy millionaire.*

The *PMA* method is not only very powerful, it's also different from *all* other existing techniques, as you will soon find out. However, if you want to know exactly why this method works and what the scientific background for it is, you can find all that information in my book called, *Desirable Power.*

The wonderful thing about *Progressive Mental Alignment* is that you don't have to learn difficult formulas, rules, behavioral patterns, or conditioning techniques. All you need to know already resides inside of you. You have only to become aware of it. Although *PMA* is a groundbreaking approach, you will be able to embrace it effortlessly. It will feel like you knew it all along, almost like coming home.

> *All you need to know already resides inside of you.*

The *PMA* concept can be used literally in all areas of life – with health or behavioral issues, in relationships, team building, management, sales, acting, etc. However, for the purposes of this book, we'll travel on one specific journey – to discover how to get rich and enjoy that wealth to the fullest.

Progressive Mental Alignment –

Regain your individuality and claim your uniqueness

Chapter 1 – It's All About Belief Systems

The nature of all humans is to desire a happy and rewarding life. So, here's the challenge: In our modern techno-driven world, how do we achieve this? A rewarding life immediately brings to mind health, wealth, and happiness. Believe it or not, you have the key to all this. Yes, one of those keys is *money*. Money is really out there in abundance and within reach of anyone that really wants it!

Becoming a millionaire is a job that requires skills, as any other profession does. There are many books, CD's DVD's, seminars and other great tools available to teach you those skills. This book is different. It is not about technical money and business *skills;* it is all about something more human – that is, *transforming* hidden inhibiting *belief systems* into proactive energy. That means opening up an exciting new path for you.

Skills for becoming wealthy are not that difficult to learn. Then why isn't everyone doing this? The answer is not because they can't learn the skills but because people tend to *sabotage themselves.* You might believe that this is due to circumstances in your environment, but by reading this book

> *It is all about transforming hidden inhibiting belief systems.*

you will discover that it's really a hidden force in your inner world that stops you from becoming successful. We all have hidden belief systems that inhibit, beliefs that work as an internal sabotage mechanism. Don't you have the desire to be rich? Well, then, why aren't you? Obviously, something in you is preventing that from happening. It can't be the world around you, because many people manage to get rich in that very same world. Therefore, if it's not something outside of you, it must be something *inside.*

That might sound disturbing at first, because you know that you truly believe you want to be rich. Don't we all? If that's your true belief, then how can an "inside job" of another belief system be stopping you? Let's be realistic; being rich is a lot more pleasant than being poor. Yet, only a few are really wealthy. How come? What stops the others, what stops you from becoming rich? There are two main reasons for that:

1. *The belief system that sabotages you is much stronger than the one that drives you to wealth.*

2. *You are not consciously aware of your own sabotaging belief systems and its origin.*

What's the importance of these belief systems in our everyday life? Well, they control everything! There's not a single decision you make that's not based on one or more of your personal belief systems – be it a small decision of minor importance, or a huge decision that will change your life radically. All these decisions are under this control. Doesn't it make sense that we need to understand the power these belief systems have and the process by which they're created? You bet it is!

> *There's not a single decision you make that's not based on your personal belief systems.*

Let's explore this idea with some concrete examples.

You wake up in the morning and you look at the clock. One belief system tells you that it is or is not okay to stay in bed for another thirty minutes. Based on that belief system you will determine what to do. You may think, *"My first business appointment is close to my home so I still have some time on my hands."* Or, *"I have to get up immediately because I have to prepare myself for this business meeting."* It's the same situation, with a totally different conclusion based on different belief systems. Here is a more important decision: You're engaged to someone you love and you have to decide: *"Will I marry him or not?"* You might believe: *"Marriage will inhibit my career and make me unhappy."* Or, *"To share my life with a soulmate like this is the fulfillment and purpose of my life!"* Two completely different outcomes based on two totally different belief systems.

Try to think of one single decision you've made that was *not* based on a belief system. I guarantee you will not find any! You cannot make a single decision unless you have an *inner drive* that will shape that decision for you. *Progressive Mental Alignment* is all about aligning your belief systems to one powerful direction – that is, to achieve success in every area of life.

> *You have to transform your inhibiting belief systems until they're perfectly aligned, pointing in the same direction.*

Do you think the belief systems of the rich are different from the poor? You can count on it! Rich people believe they have all the right in the world to be wealthy. Do you also believe you have that right? Poor people often believe that only hard manual labor can make them rich. Do you believe that too? As you will find out, these belief systems, these inner drives, totally contradict each other, preventing successful outcomes. You have to transform your inhibiting belief systems until they're perfectly aligned, pointing in the same direction.

The secret behind being rich is the transformation of *all* your inhibiting belief systems regarding money and prosperity into empowering and proactive ones. This is a lot easier to do than you might believe. However, before you can transform negative belief systems into positive ones, you have to understand how a belief system is created and what the source of its power is.

Chapter 2 – Regular Clusters and Bad Clusters

I promised that I would restrict myself to a minimal explanation about *why* things are as they are and tell you more about *how* these "things" affect you daily. You will see how you can transform these "things" from negative to positive and take a whole new direction in life. There are many books that give the scientific background, or explain the why's of the *PMA technique*, like the textbook about *PMA.*[9] But having

> *The mind and our memories are not tangibles, they are energetic information units like holograms.*

some basic knowledge about your inner processes, your physiology, and how they relate to your belief systems will give you very valuable tools to help build your successful future. These tools will allow you to understand how to transform unwanted sabotaging belief systems into motivating energy, and how to achieve the prosperity you deserve.

We all have countless memories stored as sensory data in our subconscious database. Every second of the day, our subconscious is processing parts of this data as comparison material. It is because of this that we're able to understand all the new information we receive through our five senses. We're able to think, reason, argue, make decisions and even talk to ourselves, all in our mind. Yet, even with all the present day scientific knowledge, we still don't know exactly what the *mind* is nor where it is located in our bodies. Obviously, the mind and those memories are not tangibles, even if they might

---

[9] Desirable Power: Take control of your life, health, work and relationships – by Jacob Korthuis, 2006.

feel like that sometimes. They do not consist of matter. They are, however, energetic information units, almost like holograms.

Our bodies *are* tangible and are capable of all kinds of emotional experiences. We can feel, touch, enjoy food, get sick, be damaged, and experience many other facets of life. We are able to do so exclusively based on constant physiological changes that take place in our body. The word *physiology* is a big umbrella; it covers everything in your body that moves. Think, for example, of the oxygen process, digestive system, hormonal levels, tension of muscles, thoughts, movements, blood pressure, the functioning of all the organs, like heart, liver, pancreas, thyroid, and on and on.

There are two important mechanisms in our bodies that control *all* these physiological processes:

1. *A genetic program that controls all the mechanisms that keep us alive, mechanisms like breathing and the basic functions of all our organs.*

2. *A genetic program that is exclusively operated by previously registered and stored sensory information.*

The *first* genetic program is solely designed to sustain life. It creates something we call *homeostasis*. It is the state of equilibrium, of total balance. No feelings will bother you in homeostasis; you just exist. The only "feelings" included in that genetic program are the desire for air, food, and fluid because they are necessary to sustain life and the actual homeostasis process itself.

The *second* genetic program controls all other changes in our body. This program creates all our feelings and desires. It is entirely controlled by the emotional data of previously stored experiences. This process of "learning emotions" starts as soon as our awareness, or consciousness, awakens for the first time. The only thing that's genetically pre-programmed is the ability to distinguish between pain and pleasure. This process of learning and forming feelings continues throughout our lives.

> *No one is born with particular beliefs; they are created by the experiences that life brings.*

The variances in life experiences create different feelings and beliefs for each individual. You might love the taste of sushi, while your best friend hates it. You might believe that being a vegetarian is the healthiest way of living, while your neighbor believes that all vegetarians look pale and unhealthy. No one is born with these particular beliefs and their connected feelings; they are created by the experiences that life brings. Let's elaborate this a little more:

You're looking for a new car and a car salesman manages to convince you to buy a Nissan. However, the car turns out to be a disaster. You can't even remember how many times you've had to have it repaired. After each repair, you try to convince yourself this will be the last one. *"This must be it, now the car is okay."* Finally, after a year of emotional and financial torture, you trade the car for a Mercedes. Two years later, your good friend who is very enthused about a Nissan, tries to convince you that your next car should be a Nissan. You think he must be out of his mind. You once owned a Nissan and you never, ever want to go through that disaster again!

Let me ask you a question: Is this belief sustained solely by rational facts or much more by negative emotions originating from your bad experiences with the Nissan? If it would only be rational facts, you might reason that your experience with the Nissan was probably based on just one bad car. The enthusiasm of your friend about the car clearly demonstrates that Nissan can also produce great cars. Even after having test driven your Mercedes, your friend still believes that his Nissan is the better deal.

Would you change your beliefs based on these rational arguments? You know you wouldn't. You would stick to your feelings that were created by your own (emotional) experiences with the Nissan. How and when were these feelings created? During all those times you were upset, disappointed and angry when the car needed just that one more repair. What was your mind doing during those times? Your mind was busy building a storehouse for the future, because, you see, not only were you storing the rational aspects of the damages and repairs, you were also storing the emotions you felt at that time. It's those negative emotions that helped build the negative belief system that a Nissan is not a good car and that you would never buy another one.

> *Negative beliefs are based on previous negative experiences.*

This is just one of many experiences that create our belief systems. We have five senses (hearing, sight, smell, taste, and touch) that allow us to perceive information from the external world. Usually, we are taught we have just these five senses; actually we have an important sixth.

Each of the five senses has its own external receivers or antennae (ears, nose, tongue, eyes, nerve endings) and its own specific area in the brain where all signals enter, are processed, encoded, and stored.

This becomes useful when similar data enters the brain later on. As a consequence of the similarity, new data will enter exactly the same sensory cells as previously stored similar data. This way, as a pattern evolves, all necessary comparable material is instantly available at that location to analyze and give meaning to new incoming data. It may be getting a little technical here, but as you will soon see, it will all come together just as the enhancing ingredients of a tasty dish.

> *What makes us unique is the ability to feel!*

We usually don't take into consideration that our brain processes more than just information from *outside* our bodies. Yet, it is vitally important to understand that your brain also processes information from *inside* your body. To gain information and understanding we usually focus on something, or someone, outside of our body. A sophisticated computer or robot can also do this kind of conscious information processing. However, what makes us unique at this point of the processing is that, as human beings, we have the ability to feel! This is something that completely takes place *inside* our body. It's our feelings that make us think, belief, decide, and act as humans. We're calling the information our brain receives from inside our body the *sixth sense*. This sixth sense is crucial to the process of creating awareness of our emotions, feelings and desires.

The awareness of our inner processes (our emotions) distinguishes us from lower life forms. The ability to feel is the cornerstone of our awareness. It enables us to consciously understand the world around us and make intelligent decisions, all based on our feelings. It also distinguishes us from even the most sophisticated computers and robots that cannot feel and have no awareness. While a computer merely follows programs or rational coordinates, we humans possess a conscious awareness, a conscience and a free will, all based on our feelings. Because these feelings are so very important to us, we carefully store them in our subconscious database.

This precious emotional data is not just randomly positioned somewhere in our brain. This data is thoroughly encoded and accurately stored, always connected to pieces of data that we originally perceived through our five external senses. To be able to recover the correct data and its connected feelings, the subconscious will assign two distinct neuro-physiological codes to every single peace of sensory data that enters from the outside world:

1. *The absolute code (identification code)*

2. *The relative code (emotional code)*

The *absolute code* is assigned to determine the identity of each piece of data. For instance, if I mention the word "house" you instantly know the meaning of that word. You have thousands of pictures in your subconscious database that are capable of identifying the word "house." When you see a cat you know it's not an elephant or a dolphin. Why? Because you have a lot of data in your subconscious that enables you to identify it when you see (or hear) it. In other words, we use all previously stored sensory data as comparison material to analyze and identify any incoming sensory information.

Without this huge database of absolute encoded data, you would experience every object, color, shape, sound, smell, taste, etc., as entirely new and unknown each day, again and again. It is important to understand that the assignment of the *absolute code* to identify new data is a process that is one hundred percent rational, almost mechanical. Your computer does it all the time when you enter new data. No feelings are required.

> *We use all previously stored sensory data as comparison material to analyze and identify any new incoming sensory information.*

If your brain would assign only an *absolute code* to every piece of stored data, all the pieces of data would mean exactly the same thing to you. It is the *relative code* that makes that important distinction between the similar pieces of data. This *relative code* is derived from the sixth sense. It is formed by the signals from inside your body that tell your brain how you feel about that incoming data, feelings that are delivered by your five external senses.

Thanks to this unique process, you are aware that there is a huge difference in feeling between an elephant stepping on your toe and a puppy doing the same thing to you. The elephant would scare you but being with the puppy would be fun and might even give you joy. In order to experience awareness at forty bytes per second, your subconscious has to actually process about forty million bytes per second. So, the subconscious is processing a million times more data than you will ever become aware of.

That's a huge number. Because of our feelings and this miracle of awareness, we are able to distinguish all the major differences and finer nuances of things we see, smell, taste, hear and touch every second of the day. Add to that all the times that our senses register the same object, person or situation in another context and with entirely different feelings. To illustrate this, let's look at the following example:

You have an important appointment at the office of a promising new client. He offers you a cup of coffee. However, you've just had dinner with coffee about a half hour ago. So, how important, or what is the level of feeling towards that coffee for you at that moment? It's very low and very unimportant.

Consider another scenario. You've just bought a wonderful new rug for your living room. There's a cup of coffee on the table in front of you. Your dog enters the room, excited to see you. He does not notice the coffee and, of course, the coffee ends up on your new rug. What importance or feeling does that coffee have now? Does it give you the same feeling as in the meeting with that client?

It's the same coffee, or the same data with the same *absolute code.* The major difference is in the emotional value (*relative code*). Will this affect your future behavior? What do you think? Will you put coffee on the table again the next day and let your dog in without any concern, or will you grab the dog or your cup of coffee to prevent them from colliding again? Same coffee, different response.

> *The subconscious is processing a million times more data than you will ever become aware of.*

Just consider how often you see, smell, taste, hear and touch the same things in everyday life. To be able to make an accurate distinction between the significance (feeling) of the same types of data you need more than just an identification code (*absolute code;* you need a *relative code* that provides you with an awareness through your feelings, telling you the importance and meaning of that data in each separate instance.

The *relative code* determines how you will *feel* about certain issues, people, objects, and ideas. These feelings create your belief systems which direct you to make your own conclusions and decisions, resulting in actions and behaviors that define you. *"What does all this have to do with me becoming rich?"* you might ask. Let's move forward and you will soon see that it has everything to do with it.

How did your parents feel about money and rich people? What were their belief systems that conditioned you from childhood on? The approval and recognition of our parents is of great value to us when we are young. We usually embrace their opinions because we want them to love us. This is the reason their belief systems are not just stored as rational facts (*absolute code*) in our subconscious database, but they're also closely connected to feelings (*relative code*).

In that case, it would seem that the only thing you have to do is turn the negative belief systems about money and wealth that they taught you, into positive systems, and you're done. That would seem to be a correct statement. It is indeed, as you will see, the *only thing* you have to do. But what about all these business gurus and experts that have told you pretty much the same thing so many times over, and your financial status still has not changed to your satisfaction? What is going wrong?

> *We have discovered a new phenomenon called "bad clusters."*

Methods, developed previous to *PMA* do not include the recent discovery and awareness of hidden neuro-physiological data. By connecting the most current facts in neuroscience, biology, psychology, physiology and quantum physics, we have discovered a new phenomenon called *"bad clusters."* What are *clusters* and why are some of them *bad*?

Clusters are really not bad at all. As explained before, each of your senses has its own specific area in the brain where it stores incoming information. The consequence of that is that every event we experience with our five external senses and one internal sense is stored in six different areas of the brain.

Whenever we want to remember that event, our subconscious brain collects the bits and pieces from all six areas and glues them together as one specific memory that makes sense to us. We call a memory like that a *cluster*.

Everything we've experienced and learned thus far is nicely stored in our subconscious database. We have stored every single piece of sensory information (*absolute code*) connected to the feeling (*relative code*) that was present in our body at the time of storage. We've got millions, probably billions, of these memory units stored in our subconscious database.

> *As long as we haven't lost emotional control, all the incoming sensory data will be correctly processed and encoded before it is stored.*

Normally processed and correctly encoded memories are called *clusters*. What do we mean by the phrase *"normally processed and correctly encoded"*? This refers to every event and issue that we are emotionally able to deal with, rationally and level-headedly. Consequently, we have *clusters* with positive emotional content, others with almost neutral content, and even *clusters* with negative emotional content. As long as we haven't lost emotional control, all the incoming sensory data will be correctly processed and encoded before it is stored. Our consciousness has complete access to all these properly encoded memory units.

In certain circumstances, however, our brain enters an emotional overload, like a short-circuit. During moments like these, the subconscious does *not* store *clusters* in the regularly analyzed and correctly coded way. As a result, these messages, or codes, are not available for later conscious retrieval. We call these wrongly stored *clusters*: *Bad Clusters*.

In what kinds of moments do we store *bad clusters*? We all have many of these stored moments that we've acquired over time, especially from those times when we were young and inexperienced. Whenever we were in a situation that had an intense reaction, such as panic or loss of control, for example, we created a *bad cluster*. Let's examine the following scenario:

Jake was 9 years old when he went on a vacation with his parents. To teach Jake the value of money, his parents gave him $300. The agreement was that he would not receive any additional gifts during his vacation. Whenever he wanted an ice cream, candy, toy or anything else, he had to buy it with that money. Jake was mighty proud of the independence and trust he got from his parents. On the first day of the vacation, he saw a beautiful toy that he wanted to buy that would cost him $15. He bought it and left the shop, totally focused on his new toy. Ten minutes later he wanted some candy. He reached into his pocket for his wallet and froze. Where was his wallet? He suddenly remembered that he'd left it on the counter in the store where he had bought the new toy. He ran back to the shop only to discover that his wallet with *all* his vacation money in it was gone. It felt like his world had collapsed. There was a sense of total loss, of total emptiness.

Jake created a *bad cluster* at that moment. True, that was a bad experience, but why would he store that episode so differently from that of a regular *cluster*? In what regard is a *bad cluster* so different from a regular *cluster*? Simple reason: A *bad cluster* is only created when we experience the feeling of losing control. This is an unbearable feeling for any human being. To regain that control, we try to reduce the world around us to a size that we can manage and that will give us back that extreme need to feel in control. How do we do that? By focusing and concentrating on a specific piece of sensory information. This might be a certain spot you look at, or a sound you're intently listening to, or the clinching of you fists, or holding your breath or a thousand other things.

> *A bad cluster is only created when we experience the feeling of losing control.*

After little Jake discovered his wallet was missing, the only thing he focused on was that dominant memory of his lost wallet and the money it contained. In the panicking moments that we lose emotional control, we all narrow down our world to a controllable size. The purpose of that behavior is to prevent all other incoming data from reaching our consciousness. The only thing we are able to deal with at that moment is that small piece of information that we are focusing and concentrating on. This has far-reaching consequences. How so?

Remember, every piece of incoming sensory data will always receives two codes: the *absolute code* (identification) and the *relative code* (feeling). The *relative code* represents our physiological status or our *feelings* of the moment. The *relative code* that's connected to the same piece of data can differ from event to event. Each piece of identical data is stored with its own specific *relative code* (feeling) that is appropriate for that specific context.

When Sean was a little boy, his family owned a German shepherd. He loved that animal. Today, he has many *clusters* with wonderful positive feelings (*relative code*). Carol, on the other hand, has not liked dogs since the time she was a child and was bitten by a German shepherd.

Sean and Carol are now both adults. One afternoon, they are visiting a mutual friend who owns a German shepherd. They each create a *cluster* about this visit. In those *clusters* they each store pictures of the same German shepherd. Will the dog data in Carol's *cluster* have the same *relative value* as the dog data in Sean's *cluster*? Obviously not! They each have their own specific comparison material about German shepherds, attached to very different feelings.

> *To be able to store data correctly encoded, our brain always has to compare it to previously stored similar data.*

To be able to store data correctly encoded it would always have to be compared to previously stored similar data. This comparison process provides the proper *absolute* and *relative code*. In a *cluster, all* the incoming data will be closely compared to _all_ existing _similar data_. However, during a *bad cluster* situation, you will block all unwanted incoming sensory data from entering your conscious brain and concentrate on just a *small part* of the data. *Only this part* will be correctly processed and properly stored.

What about the rest of the incoming sensory data? Well, your eyes, ears, mouth, nose, and nerves are not affected by your feelings of panic. They continue to function normally. They will deliver all the information they receive from the external world to their specific areas of the brain. The subconscious will process this information the same way it always does. It will continue to assign an *absolute* and a *relative code* to every piece of that incoming data.

The subconscious is a code reading machine, just like your computer. It will process information, assign codes, and store data. The conscious brain is tasked to shape the *relative code*. If the conscious doesn't want to do that, well, the subconscious doesn't really care. It will just assign and store

> *The subconscious is a code reading machine, just like your computer.*

the existing codes as present in the body at that time, regardless if the conscious brain shaped them correctly or not.

During normal emotional controllable events, the subconscious and the conscious brain communicate with each other at a tremendous speed to formulate and assign correct *relative codes* (feelings) for all incoming sensory data. In case of a *bad cluster* event, this communication is not possible because the conscious brain is continuously blocking all other data as unwanted. Only the small part of data that it concentrates on is allowed to enter. Consequently, the subconscious will store _all_ the other pieces of data with exactly _the same relative code._

What kinds of feelings are present in your body during a panic attack or at moments when you feel you've lost all control? Exactly, it's panic, fear! That's precisely the feeling (_relative code_) the subconscious will assign to _all_ incoming data. It has no choice but to do that, because the conscious brain does not relay its correctly shaped feelings about the data. Since the subconscious is a sophisticated computer mechanism that's genetically programmed to always assign a _relative_ and an _absolute code_ to every piece of data, it will do just that.

In a moment you will see the consequences for little Jake and how they apply to your own beliefs. So far, we've come to understand that we have a huge database in our brains and that we need this subconscious database to analyze and interpret new incoming data – in other words, to understand everyday events we need the already stored comparison material. The subconscious automatically activates and processes data that resembles the new incoming data. From your subconscious point of view, data is data, regardless whether it's found in a regular _cluster_ or a _bad cluster._

> _To understand everyday events we need similar, previously stored comparison material._

The subconscious doesn't care about the difference between the types of _clusters._ It cannot feel or think. It just reads and processes codes without judgment, just executing its genetic stimulus/response program. The activation and processing of comparison material is an automatic stimulus/response process. If there's enough similarity between the present observations and the contents of the *cluster,* then that *cluster* will become active whether you like it or not.

Our brain cells that make up the database are remarkably specific. They're only capable of storing one specific kind of data. There's one cell (or group of cells) that can only store the color blue. Another cell can only store red, and another black. In another part of the visual brain we find a cell that is only capable of storing vertical lines and another cell that stores horizontal lines. Each sensory observation is split into hundreds of thousands of these basic pieces of data. These pieces are then stored in the cells that are genetically programmed for that specific piece of data. Consequently, the subconscious has no choice but to store the data of a *bad cluster* in the very same cells as regular *cluster* data.

> *The activation and processing of comparison material is an automatic stimulus/response process.*

Unfortunately, the connected *relative code* to all the *bad cluster* data is very negative. It is loaded with the fear, panic, and pain of the *bad cluster* event. New incoming sensory data will, therefore, not only activate comparison material from regular *clusters*, but also from *bad clusters* that contain similar basic data.

Because we create *bad clusters* only when we panic or lose control, the emotions that originate from activated *bad cluster* data are very powerful and *always* negative. A *relative code* of a *bad cluster* is the highest code possible! The subconscious is genetically programmed not to ignore such high *relative codes*, regardless of their origin. Every time the *bad cluster* is activated, its physiology (that creates feelings) will be replayed and re-experienced. The problem with that is that we cannot consciously recall the *content* of the activated *bad cluster*. This same process happened to our boy Jake, when he created a *bad cluster* after the loss of his wallet. Among all the external details he observed (but banned from his conscious brain), he also experienced the *feeling* from inside his body that there was no one to help him. Not even the police was able help him.

> *The relative code of a bad cluster is the highest code possible!*

These thoughts went through Jake's mind when he walked home. His thoughts were not stored in the *bad cluster* anymore. Jake was already back on earth and able to manage his feelings. Once he was able to do that, his subconscious was able to store these other thoughts in a regular *cluster*.[10] While thinking about the loss of his money, all the mental pictures of his wallet, the shop, the toy, the shop attendant and all the other related pieces of data were automatically activated. These particular pictures contained so much data similar to the *bad cluster* that the *bad cluster* became active whenever Jake thought about what had happened. That activated the horrible *bad cluster* feelings time and again. Based on these feelings, he created a whole set of

---

[10] See Desirable Power for further explanation.

belief systems that were all empowered by this one *bad cluster*.

There's a lot more to say about how the brain processes this material and how it is possible that Jake was able to remember the event later on without activating all the negative feelings, but those are topics for another book. We'll stay with the consequences of *bad clusters* at this point and see how to transform them into positive and productive energy.

> *The problem with a bad cluster is that while we perceive something, our feelings do not match that observation.*

Although we have no awareness of the content of an activated *bad cluster*, we definitely experience the effect of its executed *relative codes* in the form of powerful negative emotions. The problem with a *bad cluster* is that while we perceive something, our feelings do not match that observation.

Joanne is at a business meeting with one of her suppliers. This supplier offers her a wonderful business opportunity. Unfortunately, the colors, shapes and sounds in the supplier's office activated one of her *bad clusters*. Now she experiences the negative physiology (feelings) of the activated *bad cluster* in her body, without any recollection of the content. She starts to sweat, her heart is pounding, and the muscles in her neck are tensing up. What is she going to do with these unexplainable feelings? She will do what we all do in such a situation – we create explanations. *"I feel sick; I must have caught some kind of virus. There must have been something wrong with the meal I had two hours ago. It is too warm in this office."*

Do you recognize her statements? They're *all belief systems!* In your attempt to manage the negative *bad cluster* feelings, as Joanne did, you will come up with "innocent" belief systems in an attempt not to damage your business opportunities. Unfortunately, many people allow these *bad cluster* feelings too create very negative inhibiting belief systems at such a moment. Often times, people create belief systems like: *"I have to be careful. I heard about many of these scams. I don't trust this guy; he's trying to deceive me. I have to rely on my gut feelings in this and get out of here!"* What if Joanne would have responded the same way as most other people? Would that have damaged her? Absolutely!

> *Bad clusters that empower belief systems are responsible for destructive behavioral patterns.*

She would have turned down that great offer. Do you recognize this scenario? Can you remember situations where you turned something down that would have benefitted you greatly? Do you remember why you turned down the offer? That's right, it was *your* belief systems.

Only belief systems that are empowered by *bad clusters* are fully responsible for these kinds of destructive behavioral patterns and also for many relationship problems, unwanted anger, unreasonable fears and *all* psychosomatic complaints. However, in the context of this book we are focusing only on the transforming of *bad clusters* driven belief systems that inhibit your abilities to become rich.

How and when are *bad clusters* created? *Bad clusters* are created during moments of intense reaction, during moments of humiliation, physical violence, rejection, betrayal, accidents, and so on. Things like being admonished by an angry parent, being locked up in a small room, receiving a shocking message, staying in a hospital, or any other of a long list of disturbing incidents, can form a *bad cluster*. Whether you create one or not differs from person to person, and from event to event. It depends on the situation, your background, constitution, health, age, and many other aspects.

It's less important at this point to understand *how bad clusters* are created, but much more important to realize *their impact* on your present life. Jake, for instance, was nine years old when he lost his wallet with all the vacation money. The emotional pain he developed from that led to some interesting personal belief systems:

> *It's extremely painful to lose money*

> *You can't trust people with regard to money*

> *Having a lot of money carries huge responsibilities*

> *People will try to steal your money*

> *It doesn't matter if you have money, you'll lose it anyway*

> *Police are of no us; they won't help you.*

Will these belief systems help Jake in becoming rich? The answer is obvious, isn't it? In his subconscious mind, having money and having the responsibility for it is connected to major pain. The destructive part of this is that the negative *bad cluster* feelings will pop up whenever he's confronted with the opportunity of making a good sum of money. He may not be consciously aware of the origin of these feelings, but when they come up, they will definitely confirm his already existing inhibiting beliefs.

If you had the same experience as Jake and had those *bad clusters* that were preventing you from becoming rich, wouldn't you agree that it's important for you to get rid of these kinds of sabotaging beliefs? Because *bad cluster* empowered beliefs are so powerful, their strength will overrule any kind of conditioning you will attempt! You'll never be able to change your belief systems with just the notion that you have to change them just by "positive thinking" or repeated endless affirmations. The hidden force of *bad clusters* is too strong for that! They will overrule any change you may try to implement. The only way to change belief systems that originate from *bad clusters* is to

> *Because bad cluster empowered beliefs are so powerful, their strength will overrule any kind of conditioning you will attempt!*

get to the root cause and transform them into motivating forces. After that process is complete, the related belief systems will automatically change.

The content of stored sensory data is not the real problem of the *bad cluster*. The real disturbance comes from the attached powerful physiology (*relative code*). The connected physiology is executed as soon as the *bad cluster* is activated. It is not activated by a similar *event* but by similarities on a very *basic level*. This is very important to understand. Because the activation is caused by incoming sensory data like a color, shape, taste, scent, facial expression, intonation of words, etc. If there is enough similarity in basic data then this could, for instance, activate a car accident of twenty years ago that was stored in a *bad cluster*. You could be attending a beautiful wedding or having a nice conversation with someone, when suddenly a *bad cluster* intervenes with its negative feelings activated by the new incoming data.

> *The content of stored sensory data is not the real problem of the bad cluster. The real disturbance comes from the attached powerful physiology (relative code).*

We cannot expect to be able to logically understand these feelings that arise at such a moment. The only thing we can be sure of is that the combination of single pieces of data in the environment at that moment has somehow served as a trigger to activate the *bad cluster*.

The original circumstances in which the *bad cluster* was created have absolutely nothing to do with the present circumstances, for it's not really the *circumstances* that activated the feelings, but a combination of particular pieces *of incoming data*. The consequence is that an activated *bad cluster* can create very negative feelings in a totally positive and fun event. Now you can also understand the source of mood swings. They suddenly appear, obviously without cause.

They don't fit the event that you're in. To make sense out of the situation, you create belief systems. Let's illustrate this important concept with another example:

> Luke invited his best friend Jeremy to his party. Jeremy had just started his own business and Luke wanted to introduce him to an elderly man who was an experienced internet marketer. This man would be able to help Jeremy in making his business flourish almost overnight.
>
> However, the moment Jeremy was introduced to the man he felt a strange, unpleasant sensation throughout his body. He instantly distrusted him. When the man offered to help, Jeremy felt resistance but had no idea why. Jeremy felt like walking away. The gentlemen told him that he would need $5,000 to market Jeremy's business properly. That was it! Now Jeremy knew why he had felt this negative vibe. He had created a group of belief systems for himself to justify why he felt this way. *This guy is a fraud. He's only interested in my money. He's not trustworthy. It would be wrong to do business with him.*

Was Jeremy right? Was it a reliable gut feeling that warned him? No, absolutely not. It was an activated *bad cluster*. Reliable gut feelings will never activate these kinds of negative fear-like vibes. What was the *bad cluster* and what activated it? Jeremy found the answer some years later when he started to use the *PMA technique*.

> Jeremy was eleven years old when he got into a fight with three older boys at school. They beat him up and scared him to the extent that he created a *bad cluster*. One of the

boys was wearing _light blue_ pants and another boy had a _grey_ shirt. They also hit him with their _brown leather_ schoolbag. It became really scary when the third guy, who was wearing a _red_ jacket, took out a _shiny knife_ and _waved it in front of Jeremy's face_.

As we see, there's no similarity in circumstances between this event from the past and the meeting with the elderly marketer. What was it that activated this particular _bad cluster_? It was activated in the same way as _bad clusters_ are always activated, based on similarities in basic incoming data and previously stored comparison material. Current _circumstances_ play no role in these activations. Jeremy's _bad cluster_ was activated because of basic similarities in data, the similarities being incorrectly encoded data loaded with the negative physiology that Jeremy experienced during his conversation with the marketer.

The elderly gentleman was wearing a _light blue_ shirt, _grey_ pants, and a _red_ tie. There was a _brown leather_ agenda on the table and the man was constantly _moving_ his _shiny_ silver pen _in front of Jeremy's face_.

Remember, every single cell in our brain has its own specific function. In this event, there's one cell being activated for the color red, but another for grey, another one for blue, and then another one for brown. Other cell combinations store the structure of leather and others the shiny metal. The underlined words in both experiences show you the similarities. The _bad cluster_ was activated among thousands of other pieces of activated _cluster_ comparison material in Jeremy's subconscious. However, the *bad cluster* data had the highest emotional value and was therefore selected.[11] It was the attached physiology of this data that created the negative reaction in Jeremy's body. This led to his belief systems that "warned him" about this man. Did this belief system serve Jeremy well?

No, not at all, as Jeremy found out soon enough. A competing entrepreneur, located just one mile away from his business, did not have the same negative beliefs about the elderly marketer and started to closely work with him. Less than a year later, the competitor's business was flourishing with six employees while Jeremy was still working alone and having a hard time to survive financially. Eighteen months after he started working with the *PMA* concept, he had a successful business with nine employees.

> *It's all a matter of your own sabotaging belief systems that stop you from becoming successful.*

Some of our very powerful belief systems are not translated into words and phrases; they're simply feelings. Just ask yourself: *"Why are so many people afraid to start their own business? Why do they feel so much resistance to sell their products and services through cold calls? Why do some find it hard to ask money for their expertise and service?"* Well, now you understand. It's all a matter of your own sabotaging belief systems that stop you from becoming successful.

---

[11] See Desirable Power for further information.

Before you found out about *Progressive Mental Alignment* you were probably not even aware of the fact that your feelings about money were *also* rooted in wrongly processed and incorrectly encoded events from your past. There is much to tell about *bad clusters* and how they determine your decisions, actions and behavior and how to turn them around to your benefit.[12] For now, we just want to continue on the journey of discovering how you can use this information towards building a wealthier future.

---

[12] For more detailed information about bad clusters, see Desirable Power.

Chapter 3 – The Origin of Belief Systems

Authentic belief systems are securely anchored in our emotions. Our personal protection mechanism makes us feel confident that our belief systems are always absolutely correct; we believe they serve us well and that they're the best for us. However, we are now aware that a large part of our belief systems originate from *bad clusters*. The emotions attached to these beliefs are extremely strong. They may have served us once and protected us during a *bad cluster* event but, in most cases, they won't really serve us well in our present daily life. On the contrary, they limit, inhibit and harm us in many ways. If you want to become rich, you have to transform these inhibiting *bad clusters* into money magnets. Otherwise, they will keep sabotaging you and forcing you to make wrong financial decisions.

Recent scientific findings have taught us that all factual sensory data *(absolute code)* is directly connected to feelings *(relative code)*. This creates new understandings of how we store and remember information. In general terms, the findings provide the following insight:

> **The more emotion we attach to sensory data, the more clearly we remember that data.**

Therefore, the more emotion that a teacher is able to connect to his teachings, the more clearly his pupils will remember what was taught. Now we understand why this is the case. It is the neuro-physiological connections between rational factual data and the emotions that offer the scientific explanation for this. Based on this understanding, we could expect the data that enters the brain during a *bad cluster* event to be remembered in every detail, since they contain the highest emotional load *(relative code)* possible.

Yet, thousands of worldwide interviews have shown that this isn't true! People that have experienced these kinds of panic events weren't able to recall many of the basic details of these highly charged events. The reason for this is that they stored these details as incorrectly encoding data in a *bad cluster*. However, even when data is stored incorrectly, the subconscious comparison and analyzing process is still able to approach the *bad cluster* data, but is totally unable to pass the contents on to the conscious brain. Why is that? That is because in order to be able to pass on data to the conscious brain, that data needs to have *correct* codes.[5] Although unable to deliver the content to the conscious brain, the subconscious can actually *read* both codes (the *relative* and *absolute code*) of the activated *bad cluster* data. It is able to recognize the extremely high *relative code* of that data. The genetic program of the subconscious doesn't allow it to ignore such a high *relative code*. Thus, a code that is this high and carries such importance will automatically be carried out by the subconscious.

> *The subconscious brain can only pass on data to the conscious brain that has correct codes.*

Why is all this so important to know in order to achieve wealth and happiness? Have you ever heard the expression: *"Knowledge is power"*? Well, the knowledge and

---

[5] For more information on this topic, see the book Desirable Power.

understanding of all this will create that foundation of power for you. Let's continue.

We're returning to the power of *bad clusters*. Keep in mind that we only create *bad clusters* during a feeling of intense emotion, when we feel we're losing control. What does this mean? We'll only panic to the point where we create a *bad cluster* if we're convinced we might lose our life or go insane. These situations activate one of the most basic feelings in a human being – *the power of survival*. In *Progressive Mental Alignment* we'll be calling this feeling *code red*. If you fear for your very existence, everything else becomes unimportant. You have to be able to live before anything else makes sense. Therefore *code red* is the highest code we know. It'll put the subconscious brain on alert instantly. Let's illustrate this with a metaphor:

> *We'll only create a bad cluster if we're convinced we might lose our life or go insane.*

You are opening your mail box and there's an envelope from the IRS staring at you. You immediately open the envelope because you know the letters I – R – S has a high relative value. You start reading the letter but, to your surprise, you realize there's no logic in the wording of the letter. It's just a bunch of randomly chosen words, without any meaning in the sentences. In other words, a correct *absolute code* (identity) has not been given. Therefore, all the words have the same relative value. This value is based on the uncomfortable feeling the letter gives you because it's from the IRS. You cannot derive a clear message from it and, as a result, its content is totally useless to you. But would you throw the letter away? Of course not! It's from the IRS. You'll carefully keep it in storage, so if the IRS contacts you later on you'll be able to prove the letter was illegible. Its high *relative code* (or emotional value) will keep you from discarding it.

An activated *bad cluster* has a similar high relative value for the subconscious. What do you think happens if you would have *bad clusters* that become activated by wealth and financial success? Do you think it would have an effect on your decisions and actions regarding money and wealth opportunities?

It's more than likely that you have some of these money and wealth related belief systems that are empowered by *bad clusters*. If not, you would already be dwelling in prosperity and enjoying it. We won't go into the neuro-physiological details of how these negative belief systems are created, but there are two characteristics that stand out:

1. *Bad clusters-rooted belief systems are* _much_ _more_ *powerful than those originating from correctly encoded clusters.*

2. *Bad clusters-rooted belief systems will never change or lose their negative power as long as you don't discover them and transform the physiological content attached to the bad cluster.*

You'll be shocked when you find out how many of your most powerful belief systems are rooted in *bad clusters* and how they empower a whole range of sabotaging belief systems. Some of them might already pop up just by reading the following questions:

> *Are you afraid of taking financial risks?*

> *Do you fear losing the money you already possess?*

> *Do you have the ability of recognizing money making opportunities and effectively investing your money?*

Keep in mind, there's an abundance of wealth and money waiting for you out there. Why aren't you utilizing that? I predict that you will discover that it's all related to your hidden inhibiting belief systems empowered by *bad clusters.*

Through the *PMA* transformation technique, the average person discovers that about 75% of *all* his negative belief systems originate from *bad clusters.* Consequently, 75% of the belief systems that the average person has about money and wealth are also empowered by that same negative source. *This explains why so many people will never achieve the level of wealth they deserve nor ever reach their full degree of potential.*

> *About 75% of all your negative belief systems originate from bad clusters.*

We all like the benefits of wealth and we all have positive belief systems about enjoying and spending it. But *positive beliefs never* come from *bad clusters.* They come from correctly encoded *clusters.* Consider this: the average person has 25% *positive* but 75% *negative* belief systems about wealth and money. Which ones will win the battle in your subconscious?

Christine had a job as a restaurant manager. She loved to cook and dreamed of running her own little restaurant. Many friends and relatives thought she was a great chef and an excellent manager. However, whenever they encouraged her to open up her own place she experienced this inner struggle. Her strong desire to move forward was constantly at war with her fearful doubts. *"I don't have enough money to pull this off. It's hard to find the right people. I can't afford to buy a restaurant at a good location. It might take years before people start knowing of my restaurant."* These and many other belief systems flashed through her mind whenever she thought about starting her own company. Were these belief systems helping her build? Did they offer her anything positive? No, and another no.

In spite of her talents and devotion she'd probably never have had her own business if it wasn't for Uncle Karl. Uncle Karl owned some nice properties in the city and he offered her a little place at a good location for a very reasonable price. Although she was still having a lot of doubts and fears, at least now she was able to move out of her stuck position. Needless to say, her hard work paid off. The restaurant took of like a rocket and has been a success ever since. After a while, Karl advised her to open up a second place and start a chain of restaurants. But, guess what? Although Christine had great skills, the right success formula and good business judgment, she now started fighting the same war of doubt all over again in her mind.

Obviously, Christine's wonderful skills weren't enough to make her a happy millionaire. Her negative beliefs inhibited her from moving into a real expansion. Even after her company became a booming business, doubts and fears kept eating at her. She simply couldn't enjoy her success. Her strong beliefs continued to attack her emotionally. Eventually, she became severely depressed and had to start on medication.

After some time, she discovered the *PMA* belief system transformation technique and started studying and applying it with a PMA Coach. She was stunned when she discovered several *bad clusters* that had prompted her fears and doubts for so many years. Her depression disappeared instantly, together with her doubts and inhibiting beliefs. A few months later, she opened up a second restaurant and six weeks after that, a third. Christine is now on her way to becoming a happy millionaire. What a waste of talents and potential it would have been if Christine wouldn't have traced and transformed her *bad clusters* into proactive power.

You will not be able to transform your doubts and sabotaging fears as long as you don't know where to look and what to look for! That's why you need this basic knowledge of understanding how the brain processes information. Then you can understand what the consequences are if something goes wrong and how that creates negative emotions and inhibiting belief systems. The results you achieve by applying the *PMA Transformation Technique* will continue to fascinate you.

Very soon, you'll learn about all the other areas of life in which *PMA* is also a powerful tool.[6]

Let's continue to focus on the practical application of *PMA* with regard to money. How can you find the roots of your belief systems about wealth and money? Money related belief systems are usually easier to trace than other issues. Why? We simply have no legitimate reason for having *any* negative belief system about wealth and money. So, any negative belief you have must originate from *bad cluster* data.

> *You will not be able to transform your doubts and sabotaging fears as long as you don't know where to look and what to look for!*

We're living in a world (yes, even a universe) of abundance. There are overflowing amounts of money and opportunities to becoming rich. Most people don't get them though, because they're driven by lots of negative sabotaging belief systems about money. Do these statements sound familiar?

- *Money leads to corruption.*

- *Getting rich means abusing others.*

- *You're never safe when you're rich (stealing, kidnapping).*

- *Wealth brings sorrow.*

- *Money is the root of all evil.*

---

[6] For more information about books, CD's, DVD's and seminars, visit www.pmainstitute.com

> *If I'm rich I will lose my friends and family.*

> *People will be jealous if I'm rich.*

> *People will try to abuse and manipulate me to benefit from my wealth.*

> *It's difficult to attain and maintain wealth.*

> *The responsibility of wealth is a heavy burden.*

> *Friends will only like me for my money.*

These and many more belief systems control the lives of the majority of people. Most negative belief systems originate from *bad clusters*, but some might be rooted in *clusters* loaded with negative emotions. These might, for example, have been created by the opinion of our parents. Belief systems that come from negatively charged *clusters* change easily after we receive new positive information that will contradict and remove the potency of the old beliefs. When addressing these beliefs, the attached *clusters* will instantly and spontaneously come to mind. Belief systems empowered by *bad clusters*, however, are totally different. They are not admissible to rational arguments. You first have to find the content and origin of the *bad cluster* before any attached belief system, action, thought, or anything else can change.

> *You first have to find the content and origin of the bad cluster before any attached belief system, action, thought, or anything else can change.*

How do you recognize the difference in origin of a belief? That's easy. If a belief system is rooted in *clusters* you can instantly and easily trace it back to the why, how, and when of its formation. Just remember, *clusters* are correctly encoded memories and your consciousness has normal access to them. *Bad clusters* are just the opposite. You cannot simply remember them. Let's do a little exercise to find out if you are able to trace back your belief systems easily or not. Ask yourself:

> ➢ *What are my most important beliefs about money and wealth?*

After you found one of your negative belief systems, ask yourself questions like:

> ➢ *Why do I believe this?*

> ➢ *Who taught me these belief systems?*

> ➢ *What was the first time this belief showed up?*

> ➢ *What experiences confirmed this belief as true?*

You need to follow your feelings about these questions and not just go with rational thoughts. Beliefs are not created by rational thinking but are always rooted in emotions! Our most powerful belief systems are usually created early on in our life. They often don't even have words assigned to them. They exist only as feelings.

If a belief system is rooted in *clusters,* you will easily remember where it comes from. Tracing it back will not cause you discomfort. If it's empowered by a *bad cluster*, you will increasingly feel uncomfortable by questioning it. You can instantly and easily change all your belief systems about money and rich people that are based on *clusters* after you receive convincing information that contradicts the existing beliefs.

In short, belief systems based on *bad clusters:*

> ➤ *cannot simply be traced back to their origin*

> ➤ *cannot simply be changed*

> ➤ *will make you feel uncomfortable when you're questioning their legitimacy*

> ➤ *need the* PMA *technique to be able to trace and transform them*

The exercise I mentioned above is even more effective if you do it with your partner or with your friends. They usually have a more objective vision about your belief systems than you do. This usually results in additional questions that *you* might avoid asking yourself. Start with telling them your belief systems, then have them ask you as many questions as they can about the origin and reason you believe that.

> Mike wanted to try this exercise because he was convinced he didn't have the skills to become rich. *"I simply don't know how to pull it off!"* His wife, Jamie, was willing to help him with the exercise and asked: *"Why do you believe that?"* He responded: *"You know my father is a real good businessman. He keeps*

reminding me that I don't have it in me. He's told me time and again that I will never become a businessman because I never see the opportunities to make easy money." Jamie replied: *"Oh really, and how do you feel about his opinion?"* *"I feel okay with that, I have no specific feelings about it. He's probably right."* Jamie reacted surprised: *"What about the other day when you saw this motorcycle and you bought it? You didn't need or want a motorcycle but because of its low price you immediately said it was an opportunity to make money. Within three days, you made $1,400 profit on that bike. Did you forget?"* Mike immediately responded: *"That's nothing, I was just lucky."* Jamie looked at him and her jaw dropped: *"Oh, really? So you didn't see the opportunity? What about when we bought our first house? I wanted the other home, but you convinced me we wouldn't be able to sell it so easily if we wanted to move after a while. You instantly saw that the house we decided to buy was in a better location and had better upgrading opportunities with just a little investment. You said we would be able to sell it with a nice profit and you were right. We made $45,000 on that house within eighteen months! Why are you holding on to that stupid belief system your father's trying to enforce on you?"* Mike started to laugh: *"Wow, you're serious about this, aren't you?"* *"You bet I am. Just think of these two opportunities you instantly recognized. I can even come up with more if you like. Do you still think your father's right?"* Mike smiled and he started to feel different about his business skills.

Mike was able to change this particular belief without any discomfort. All he needed was some positive input that showed his beliefs were wrong. This particular belief was surely rooted in *clusters* created during his upbringing and planted by the opinion of a man he respected. He never doubted the opinion of his father in this matter, until the moment his wife started to use a few aspects of the *PMA belief system transformation technique* on him.

It's actually interesting, mostly even fun, for partners to practice this exercise together. It can bring you closer to each other and give you some real eye-openers about yourself. It will also prepare you for the application of the next steps of the *PMA technique*. Let's continue our discovery journey. After every belief system you found, just ask the following questions:

> *Does this belief system serve me beneficially?*

> *Does it motivate me to become rich?*

> *How can I transform this belief system into one that really motivates me to become rich?*

> *Would I like to change my beliefs and rules about money?*

> *If the answer is no, why not?*

> *If the answer is yes, what is stopping me from making the necessary changes?*

> ➤ *During which moments do I want to hold on to that new belief system?*

Once again: If the belief system originates from negative *clusters* containing impractical information, you can change them easily and quickly. The only thing you need is a more objective view and positive, constructive arguments. You will find comfort, trust, and a positive feeling in applying your newly created positive beliefs. When you try and change belief systems empowered by *bad clusters* you will react differently. After rephrasing these beliefs into positive ones, you will instantly feel resistance when you apply them. You'll automatically return to the old beliefs that dictated your decision and behavior before. This inability to hold on to your new belief system is actually another clear sign that the old negative belief originates from *bad clusters*.

> *Only a few bad cluster empowered beliefs are enough to sabotage your whole financial future.*

The sum of your belief systems creates the underlying blueprint of *all* your decisions and actions. Even if you have a large amount of positive belief about wealth and money, only a few *bad cluster* empowered beliefs are enough to sabotage your whole financial future. You will always act according to your most powerful beliefs. None of your *cluster* driven belief systems will ever reach the level of power of those that have their roots in a *bad cluster*! If your belief systems are driven by negative *bad cluster* emotions, then what can you expect from your decisions and actions that you base them on? Here is the simple truth, in a well-known phrase:

> *If you think what you've always thought, and if you do what you've always done, you'll receive what you've always received.*

If you want to transform your life and enter the realm of abundant wealth and happiness, you have to take the first step — that is, actively transform the sabotaging, inhibiting belief systems into those that will bring you success and total fulfillment.

Chapter 4 – Your Safe Place

Now it's time for our next step. Once you understand that 75% of your belief systems are empowered by unknown subconscious comparison material, we can start with your *belief system transformation program*. The process is easy and a lot of fun once you understand it. Try to be open-minded about what you are about to read because you'll definitely discover some new, exciting information. Let's first take a look at how modern science describes our different types of awareness:

> *About 75% of your belief systems are empowered by consciously unknown comparison material.*

> ➢ *The awareness created by the information our senses gather from the external world.*

> ➢ *The awareness created by our ability to* think *rationally about information, which leads to reaching conclusions and taking certain actions.*

> ➢ *The awareness created by our feelings.*

> ➢ *The awareness created on a holographic intuitive level.*

So far, we've discussed some important background information about the first three levels. Now, we will focus on the last one, our *holographic intuitive level* of understanding. This is the next step in bringing you closer to the fulfillment of your dreams of wealth.

Our *holographic intuition* comes in many shapes and sizes. You don't have to learn or accomplish anything to acquire it. We *each* have this awareness in us and only need the proper information to understand how to use it. Once you have this valuable realization it will serve you well for the rest of your life. In addition, you will experience it as an indispensable aspect of your journey to prosperity.

Some people are able to approach this realm of awareness at a high level, others at a lower level and some might not use their *holographic intuition* at all. Since we all possess the innate capacity to approach this realm, it's a matter of <u>your own choice</u> whether to do so or not. To explore this exciting and beneficial level of awareness we have to follow a few easy steps.

The first step is to create a *safe place*. If you want to grow and transform your sabotaging belief systems into proactive and motivating powers you need a place that's quiet, where no one will disturb you. It's necessary to come to a relaxed state in order to arrive at the full awareness of *all* your positive and inhibiting beliefs regarding money and wealth. Sometimes, our hectic lives make. this task very difficult. The wonderful thing about the *PMA transformation technique* is that your *safe place* does not depend on a physical location.

> *Your safe place does not depend on a physical location. You create your own quiet safe place within your mind.*

You create your own quiet *safe place* within your mind; it's an imaginary place. It's not a tangible physical place but it exists in the sub-atomic holographic world, in the energy waves of your brain. Nobody can ever disturb you there if you don't allow it. You can go there whenever you want and stay as long as you want. Although imaginary, it has to feel very real to you. You really have to experience total comfort and safeness there.

Why is a *safe place* like that so important? Try to remember a moment in your life when you felt totally safe and serene. This can be any safe and quiet place, like a vacation spot or anything else that works for you. When you're in this safe place, nothing should be able to bother you – no negative emotions, no disturbing thoughts. Are these not the moments when we have great ideas, moments of enlightenment? We suddenly know the answer to problems that, a few moments ago, seemed like huge roadblocks. How come? When we feel safe and calm, our total database is accessible without being inhibited by any rational or emotional restraint. We enter *another state of awareness*. That's exactly the purpose of the *safe place*, to go into a *relaxed state of consciousness* to make your total database accessible.

In this *safe place* your thoughts can flourish without all kinds of hindering belief systems. You are one with yourself and you're allowing your subconscious brain to come up with any thought or impulse it wants to. It's not important whether this *safe place* is a room, beach, mountain, air-balloon, or any place in the universe. All it has to be is a place where you feel entirely safe and comfortable.

It's usually very easy to imagine a place like this. Nevertheless, some people find it a little difficult to create their personal quiet and safe place. If you're one of them, try this:

> *Picture the most relaxing color in your mind.*

> *Hear the most relaxing music in your mind.*

> *Taste your most favorite meal.*

> *Feel your most comfortable chair.*

> *Smell the most pleasant smell.*

> *Try to enjoy each of these sensory experiences.*

> *Combine all of them to create a specific place in your mind.*

> *Go with that location if it feels right. If not, continue combining all these sensory aspects until you spontaneously come up with a place that works.*

> *When you've found your specific location, see, hear, feel, smell, and taste that safe place to become totally familiar with it.*

Once you have your *safe place* established, the real transformation process can begin. Now you will go on a journey to transform your negative belief systems into sources of positive energy. Its motivational effect will free your full potential. Human nature needs to feel and believe that we're in control. Your safe place is an important step to let you feel *you are* in control of your inner world at *all* times. The more control you gain over your inner world, the easier it becomes to control the outer world and your behavior in it.

Chapter 5 – Your Higher Self

We've all experienced moments in life when we have had to make a decision about something and, deep down we knew the decision wasn't going to be the correct one. We repeatedly refuse to listen to these gut feelings. We prefer to listen to our irrational arguments and emotions and blindly follow what we _want_ to believe. Sure enough, some time later our gut feeling proves to be right and we're blaming ourselves once again for not listening to it. Do you recognize these moments in your own life? Some might call it a gut feeling, others intuition, a sixth sense, or instinct.

The question is: Where do these impulses come from? Why is it that deep down, we _know exactly_ what to do at moments like these? It's not important what you want to believe about the origin of these gut feelings. Important is: We _all_ recognize them and we _all_ have them! It's not something we only experience once in a lifetime. No, we experience these gut feelings many times over and over, even on a daily basis. If you don't want to believe any of the given scientific and non-scientific explanations, then don't, but at least _believe yourself_ and what _you_ experience in your own mind and body. Once you experience the benefits, you'll absolutely need and want to start exploring. You'll want to stay in touch with this level of awareness because it will unmistakably guide you to prosperity.

> _You'll want to stay in touch with this level of awareness because it will unmistakably guide you to prosperity._

Some will argue "gut feelings" come from our life experiences, education, culture and conscience or, from our subconscious comparison material. Others might say they're caused by the fact we're made in the image of God. And because we're still a reflection of Him at some level, we know deep down what's right and what's wrong. Then there are the quantum physicists, they tell us we're all connected because everything that we call matter is made out of pure energy waves and vibrations. Some quantum physicist will say this gut feeling is your counterpart in hyperspace,[7] your perfect blueprint with unlimited potential. Then there are the medical scientists who try to convince us it's all a matter of biochemical reaction in your brain and body.

You don't need to go into any of these points of view. You have *your* answer, *your* truth, already inside of you. The only thing you have to do is allow it to come to the surface. It'll be a great experience to discover how you can easily approach this level of awareness and how you can consciously use it in *all* matters of life. In *PMA* we call this deep gut feeling *"your higher self."*

Science teaches us we're made of energy and are all connected, not only with everything on earth but also with everything in the universe. The following explanation will show you that the concept of a *higher self* isn't just a fairytale-like story but that it finds its roots in serious science. It'll help you trust and understand *your higher self* as a reality once you start working with it.

---

[7] Hyperspace is the force outside our universe where time and space don't exist and all matter in our entire universe originated.

Science tells us that our bodies and all matter around us, consist of billions of atoms. The building blocks of these atoms are basically energy vibrations. To understand the complex insights of this in an easier way, you can compare our existence with something on your television screen. When an object or a person is moving on your TV, it's not physically present on your screen. It's just an *image* created by dots of energy in different colors and locations. These dots lighten up and disappear, giving you the impression that the object or person is moving. Although this is a two-dimensional process and we're living in a three-dimensional world, in essence, there isn't much difference between the images on your television screen and us as a part of the universe.

Basically, we (and the whole universe around us) are just a bunch of atoms that vibrate and constantly move at an incredible speed, in and out of existence. What force is controlling this unique mechanism? We can understand how scientists explain this if we stick to our metaphor of the television set.

A television set is able to produce sound and pictures. To do that, it needs input. To create the final moving picture it needs seven elements. You'll find the human equivalent in parenthesis:

➢ An intellectual creative source *(your higher self)*

➢ A broadcasting station *(hyperspace)*

➢ Waves to transport the image *(the energetic atomic structure of the universe)*

➢ Electricity to be able to function *(life force, Chi)*

➢ Antennae to receive the waves *(our cell receptors)*

➢ Video equipment to store information *(our subconscious brain)*

➢ Machinery to translate the waves into sound and picture *(body, ligands, hormones, energetic impulses)*

A television set receives information but cannot independently create and send messages back to the broadcasting station. It's a *one-way* communication process. Of course, there are major differences between a TV and a human being. We can *feel,* we have *free will,* we have *consciousness,* and we can *plan* things. Because we are aware of our existence, we're able to intellectually create independent conclusions, questions, ideas, etc. and send them back to the broadcasting station. We, as people, use *two-way* communication.

A television set wouldn't be able to function without electricity and waves. Both concepts are invisible energy. They both need an intelligent source to produce and send them. Humans also need a body *(a television)*, electricity *(life force/Chi)*, and intelligent input via waves of information *(higher self/hyperspace)*. If the wave of information *(the broadcast)* stops, the television cannot receive or produce pictures or sound. Scientists believe the entire universe (which includes you and me) needs a similar intelligent "broadcasting" input in order to keep its energy waves *(its energetic atomic existence)* active for our physical bodies. In essence, we do not consist of matter, but of *energy vibrations*

formed as matter. Just think of your thoughts and imaginations. They're not tangible; they are clearly a result of *energy vibrations.* These holographic vibrations are being kept alive by our consciousness. How is that done?

Our atoms are arranged in a way that we perceive our brain and the rest of our body as matter. However, our mind is definitely not tangible. It's purely energetic, purely holographic. With all the scientific knowledge of the world at our side, we still don't exactly understand how our awareness comes into existence and what exactly our *mind* is. The more we learn about the laws of the universe, the more scientists believe in a *unified force field* as the earliest origin for all things. There's no space and time in this force field, everything is totally connected to everything else.

It is beyond our human understanding to know what this force field is made of and how it can exist without space and time. It's even stranger considering the increased amount of scientific facts that we know or are able to perceive about everything originating from that force field. You might say: *"I don't care if I understand the laws of the universe and I don't need to understand it. For me this force field is totally clear, this field is God!"* One thing is for sure, whether you call it God or the *unified force field* or any other name, it is a realistic power source that will help you to become successful if you allow it.

Whether the foregoing explanation is correct or just a figment of scientists, whether our behavior is entirely biochemically controlled, the product of evolution or creation, the result of genetic programs connected to stored life experiences, or a physical reflection of *your higher self*, one thing is evident: We are here, we live, we think, we feel, and we are conscious beings.

The good thing is, you don't need faith in any of the above belief systems to experience the power of *your higher self*. The only thing you need is an open mind, being able to unlock your innate capacity to imagine. You'll meet *your higher self* and discover that it knows *exactly* what you need to do to become rich and happy.

> *You don't need faith to experience the power of your higher self. The only thing you need is an open mind.*

Your higher self is the energetic reflection of you, or maybe even more correctly said: You are the physical expression of *your higher self*. It's you in its purest form with endless potential. It's *all* you can be if you allow yourself to grow to the highest level without inhibiting belief systems. *Your higher self* has no inhibiting factors or sabotaging belief systems at all. It is your personal mirror of truth. Its intentions are *always* pure and good. *Your higher self* is *always* there for you, to help you whenever you need. Let's see how you can get to know and communicate with *your higher self*.

Chapter 6 – Communicate with Your Higher Self

How can you meet *your higher self?* You've probably already met many times, but were unaware of it. Every time your "gut feeling" told you what was right and what was wrong, you were in contact with *your higher self.* That self always knows what's best for you. This is what you need to do to intensify this beautiful level of awareness:

> ➤ *Go to your safe place in your mind*

> ➤ *Imagine yourself as an energetic being with endless potential*

Follow your gut feeling (*holographic intuition*) 100% in this process. Don't start reasoning or thinking! Close your eyes and just experience what will happen. Allow your mind to do whatever it wants. After they read this, most people instantly experience an image of their *higher self.* Some see an image of light; others see themselves in a perfect shape, some see themselves in shiny clothes. Make it as real as possible. There's no textbook to tell you how *your higher self* should appear. Things are as they are, that's how easy it is.

Very few people have problems imagining their *higher self.* Those who do find it difficult usually make the mistake of approaching the whole concept too rationally. You cannot approach *your higher self* through a line of reasoning. This whole process takes place on another level of awareness. Your mind and *your higher self* are entirely energetic and holographic. They don't appear in the rational realm. Their capacities go way beyond that. If you are having some difficulty in consciously connecting to *your higher self* this is what you can do:

> *Find a quiet location where nobody will bother you.*

> *Close your eyes and go to your safe place.*

> *Walk and look around in your safe place until you feel totally safe and relaxed.*

> *Find a comfortable chair in your safe place and relax until you reach the feeling of a daydream.*

> *Imagine how you would look as a perfect energized being. You have no flaws and you have endless potential.*

Once the image of *your higher self* is present, take your time to become fully acquainted with this image. Realize that *your higher self* doesn't exist in a physical realm but in an *energetic holographic realm* of awareness. There are no limitations, no inhibiting belief systems in *your higher self*. Let's take the next steps to make you feel more familiar with the conscious presence of *your higher self*.

> *Look at your higher self for a while to become more consciously aware of its appearance.*

> *Place yourself and your higher self in your safe place.*

> *Approach your higher self and embrace it.*

> *Take your time and become fully aware of the effect this energetic bond has on you.*

You are now ready to start communicating. This can be done with a real conversation inside your head, but sometimes it might just be a flash, an impression, a feeling, all faster than the speed of light. *Your higher self* has an enormous capacity of producing answers and has an abundance of dynamic energy. Sometimes you'll present a problem to *your higher self* and you'll instantly know the answer, even without one word of communication.

Don't just talk to *your higher self,* embrace it. Become aware of the trust and feel the power. You can share all your sorrows and pleasures and ask every question you want. *From now on, you'll never be alone again.* You can communicate about everything that's on your mind, whenever you want, wherever you want. Discussions are not restricted to financial things. You'll be surprised to find out how much good advice and benefiting strategies *your higher self* has in store for you. The only thing you have to do is ask with an open mind.

From now on, you'll never be alone again. The only thing you have to do is ask with an open mind.

Once again: this whole process doesn't take place on a rational level. It goes even more deeply than your standard emotions. It's on a *holographic intuitive* level, another level of awareness.

Let's continue:

> *Start a conversation with your higher self about whatever subject you want.*

> *Ask your higher self how he perceives you.*

> *What does your higher self recommend that you to do in order to work on your personal development?*

> *What are the most important steps you have to take at this point in your life to feel good about yourself and be successful?*

Take your time for this process. The answers usually come quickly. Return to your *safe place* on a daily basis, several times a day, to communicate with *your higher self* about your feelings, decisions and behavior. Once you're totally used to being in the conscious presence of *your higher self* and you've developed the habit of communicating about every decision you make, you can start focusing on your future financial possibilities. You can ask questions like:

> *What are the first changes I have to make to create a successful financial future?*

> *What are my weakest points with regard to money issues?*

> *What do I have to do to overcome those weaknesses?*

You can ask these and many other questions, especially the ones that personally bother you and sabotage your reaching the highest level of your financial abilities. *"So, if I just ask my higher self, I will get all the correct answers, and when I*

act on them will I be successful? Is that all I have to do?" That's right, and I know that you'll be surprised about some of the answers you'll get.

We're not done yet; the fun has just started. Remember the explanation about *bad clusters?* Well, they're in this book for a very good reason, as you'll find out in the following chapters!

> *From now on you'll never have to do it alone! You'll always have your higher self as your safe and powerful companion.*

One of the most important realizations of this chapter is that *from now on you'll never have to do it alone!* You'll always have *your higher self* as your safe and powerful companion, always there for you; not just for financial matters but for anything you want to communicate.

Chapter 7 – Your Friend Mechanism

The conscious awareness of *your higher self* will now become a part of your discovery tour. Before we take the next exciting step in this transformation program, let's discuss a very important mechanism that we all have. In *PMA* language we call it your *"Friend Mechanism."*

If you would have to describe a perfect friend, what would he be like? Do you have a notion of what makes a perfect friend? Most people have. We usually know how a perfect, reliable friend would act. Where does this knowledge come from?

Each of us has a built in protection mechanism. It's a mechanism that operates on all levels: biological, rational, physiological, and emotional. It will always make the *most positive* subconscious *connections* between one cell and another, one memory and another, one energetic field and the next, one thought and the next. The purpose of these connections is always driven by positive intentions. Most connections take place on a biological and on a holographic subconscious level.

Your *friend mechanism* always follows the strict rules of the subconscious language and is driven by your most powerful innate force:

Away from pain

Whenever your *friend mechanism* reads a *relative code* (emotion) that expresses pain, fear or danger, it will always push you as far away from it as possible. That means, you will

---

be pushed away from emotions in the present, but also from pain and fear of the past. Your *friend mechanism* is a very powerful system. Under normal circumstances, it is responsible for preventing you from burning yourself with a hot pan or from falling off a cliff; it helps you choose your words carefully to avoid unnecessary reactions.

Your *friend mechanism* is the control center of your belief systems. Belief systems are always based on your innate drive *away from pain* (or more often the choice between *pain* and *less pain*). If you would have a perfect body that flawlessly analyzed, encoded and stored all events and neuro-physiological data (*clusters*), all your belief systems would be perfect. They would *all* serve you in *all* circumstances.[8]

You now know about the disrupting influence of *bad clusters* on more than 75% of all your belief systems. The feelings originating from those *bad clusters* are very powerful. That's why we are so convinced about the correctness of *our* belief systems, especially the ones empowered by *bad clusters*. Here's the shocking news:

> ➤ *None of the belief systems empowered by bad clusters are positive!*

> ➤ *None of those belief systems serve you at this time!*

> ➤ *All bad cluster driven belief systems inhibit you from becoming successful!*

---

[8] See the book Desirable Power for more information about the *friend mechanism*.

Your *friend mechanism* will do anything to hide painful *bad cluster* data from your awareness. *"But if they're cloaked by my conscious brain then I'm hopelessly lost,"* you say. No, on the contrary! Finally, you'll be able to trace and release the full potential you've hidden in these *bad clusters* for the very first time. That's incredible news!

> *Finally, you'll be able to trace and release the full potential you've hidden in these bad clusters for the very first time.*

Don't stop now; keep reading. We'll show you exactly how to discover your *bad clusters* and transform their inhibiting belief systems into proactive energy. Just follow the procedure as described in here and ask *your higher self* to advise and guide you in the process. Get ready; you're on your way to experience unbelievable things.

Bad clusters are imprisoning enormous amounts of energy, which in turn empower the related belief systems. This huge amount of energy will be liberated as soon as one or more *bad clusters* is found and transformed, free to be used for enriching plans and deeds. When you've discovered the content of a *bad cluster* you'll instantly feel relieved and full of energy, in a matter of seconds. No difficult procedures or repetitive behavioral rituals needed. The only thing you have to do is trace the origin of a *bad cluster* and the transformation will automatically take place in your subconscious at a tremendous speed. It's a one-time process. Every *bad cluster* you discover will be transformed into positive energy forever. Each will add power to your drive in reaching your goals of becoming rich.

Your *friend mechanism* will work perfectly in your behalf as long as you are dealing with events in your life that you are emotionally able to handle. In *bad cluster* situations, however, the code-reading machinery of your *friend mechanism* isn't powerful enough to avoid pain beyond an acceptable level. This is when we escape to the *holistic energetic world* in our mind, because we no longer want to be a part of our body that's in panic or distress. When you are in this untouchable energetic world you can actually look at yourself and watch from a safe distance.

> *Every bad cluster you discover will be transformed into positive energy forever.*

Although this *holistic world* is in the same realm where *your higher self* resides, this escape definitely isn't the same as contacting *your higher self*. This escaping process takes place at the other end of the spectrum. You're not entering the endless potential realm of *your higher self*; you're just using a *very tiny part* of your *holistic energetic world* to escape. So, instead of using your endless potentials here, you're *restricting* yourself to using the incomplete aspect of safety. Let's look at an illustration of this concept:

Jenny adored her grandfather. But when she was five years old she saw him fall to the floor and die of a heart attack. Everybody in the room panicked, nobody paid any attention to her. Little Jenny was unable to deal with these strong emotions and her brain went into overload – she created a *bad cluster*. To reclaim her control she started focusing on a painting on the wall of the living room.

There was a field of grass, and a little girl playing with flowers. Jenny escaped to the painting and started playing with the girl.

At this point, Jenny wasn't escaping to her *higher self* but she was going to an escape place in the *holistic energetic world*. In psychological terms, Jenny was dissociating. Her mind placed itself completely outside of her body. We all have this ability; it's a normal part of our genetic program. It's not important whether you want to believe this process happens inside the brain or if we're really able to step outside of our body. The result is the same: preventing uncontrollable fear and distress.

Emotion can only be perceived through the mechanisms of our physical body. During moments of dissociation, however, you're not residing in your physical body anymore; you're in the *holistic energetic world* of your mind. Therefore, your non-physical mind is not receptive to negative emotions or experiences of pain.

> *Emotion can only be perceived through the mechanisms of our physical body. Your non-physical mind is not receptive to panic.*

When she was an adult, was Jenny not aware that her grandfather had died when she was five? Of course she was. Her family had even told her she was there when it happened. Jenny certainly believes them but she has no recollection of the event herself. She stored most of the event in a *bad cluster* and in several other *clusters* right after the *bad cluster*. On top of that, her *friend mechanism* started suppressing the data of those particular *clusters* soon after the event. She couldn't even remember attending her grandfather's funeral, although her parents said she did. You might say, that the grandfather's death had nothing to do with money. That couldn't be what was sabotaging Jenny's plans for getting rich. Well, let's see what happened to Jenny when she was in her twenties:

Jenny had been working at a nice clothing store for three years now. The owners of the store were an elderly couple without children. They loved Jenny like a daughter. One day, they invited her over and told her they wanted to retire. They made Jenny the very profitable offer of taking over the business for 70% of its real value. She didn't even have to worry about the mortgage because they'd leave their money in the business and let her have it for a very low rate. Jenny instantly felt very uncomfortable when she heard the unbelievable offer, but was touched by their offer and trust. She loved her work and would really like to stay on but she also felt a tremendous discomfort. It made her very insecure. She thanked them asked if it was okay to think about it for a while.

While driving home through a beautiful *green landscape* with lots of *wildflowers,* Jenny's uncertainty and resistance to accept the offer became even stronger. A whole list of belief systems popped up: *"I can't handle this responsibility. I'm too young for this. I won't have any private time once I own the business. I'll have to work too hard. The responsibilities won't allow me to enjoy life and will finally make me sick or even kill me."* What should she do? Should she accept this great offer or not?

Well, you guessed right, she didn't accept the offer. Fear, originating from her own sabotaging beliefs, stopped her. Can you imagine how surprised she was to find out that her grandfather's death caused all these negative beliefs? Let's see what she discovered:

> In the hours following her grandfather's death, little Jenny became very sad. She started to realize she'd never see grandpa again. Family members were starting to come to the house and talk about what happened. These are some of the statements and beliefs that Jenny heard: *"It's so sad, he was on the verge of retirement, and now this happens. He could finally start enjoying life and now he's dead. His company killed him, I'm sure of it. He was always working too hard. He was much too young to die!"*

When these things were said, Jenny wasn't in a *bad cluster* mode anymore. So, all the things she heard were stored in *clusters*. Was she able to remember these words when she was an adult? No, she wasn't. Do you recall your most powerful drive? Right, *away from pain*! Her *friend mechanism* took care of suppressing the painful memories.[9] But this doesn't stop the subconscious from activating the *clusters* as comparison material. The subconscious would still use them; it just won't deliver the content to your consciousness and make you aware of them.

Why would Jenny suppress the memories? Consciously remembering the content of the *clusters* would bring her right back to the living room where it all happened. This would

---

[9] See Desirable Power for details on how we suppress this.

bring up all the details of the room, which would immediately activate the *bad cluster*. The attached *relative codes* would cause too much pain and sadness. So, her *friend mechanism* suppressed the *clusters* and hid their content for her consciousness.

Jenny was stunned when the *PMA technique* revealed the similarities between her grandfather's death and the elderly couple's offer. She even saw the resemblance between the grass and the flowers on the painting and the landscape she saw from her car when she drove home after receiving the incredible offer. Jenny soon figured out how she had created her own inhibiting belief systems. Every single one of her beliefs was related to what her family had said the day grandpa died. Of course, statements like "he was too young" weren't only made just after his death. She'd heard them many times after that in all kinds of situations.

Whenever Jenny heard one or more of these remarks, very specific words were activated in her database, including those uttered right after grandpa's death. This, in turn, instantly activated the related *clusters* and (through them) the *bad cluster* with its powerful physiology. The beliefs felt so right when she heard them. It even scared her to think it could be any other way. But after she'd transformed the energy of the *bad cluster* into a positive power, all the related belief systems collapsed and made way for healthy proactive ones that helped her expand her financial potential.

The *holistic energetic world* you escape to during a *bad cluster* event is the same world where you meet with *your*

higher self. In other words, you're creating a flash of awareness on an entirely different level when you're in a moment like this. When the period of pain, fear and distress is over, you'll become fully aware of your physical existence again. As in Jenny's case, the existing pain, fear and distress will not be instantly gone. There's still a moment when you're partially in this dissociated state, but at the same time you're also in awareness of your body. It's almost like slowly waking up from a bad dream. You're returning to your body at the very moment that you're capable again of dealing with the existing emotions and processing them in a normal way.

Have you ever had a car accident or received a shocking message? Then you're familiar with the feeling of numbness for a few seconds after it. You don't even consciously notice it until your awareness returns.

> *A Bad Cluster is not spontaneously accessible to your conscious brain.*

When your mind's completely wrapped up in this state of dissociation, you create a *bad cluster.* However, the data about that moment is not just stored in a *bad cluster.* It's also stored in the *cluster* created right after that, during that tiny moment of awakening, between being dissociated and being fully returned to your body. This 'overpass' moment is normally processed and correctly encoded, so it's stored as a *cluster.* In other words, now there's a part that's *not* spontaneously accessible (*bad cluster*) to your conscious brain and another part that *is* accessible (*cluster*).

The accessible part is loaded with large amounts of data resembling the data in the *bad cluster*. In reality, you're still with the same people at the same location right after the dissociated moment. So, whenever this specific *cluster* is activated, its related but incorrectly encoded big brother, the *bad cluster*, will also be activated. This happens because the subconscious brain is an automated stimulus/response machine that has no choice. There are simply too many similarities between the contents of the *bad cluster* and the *regular cluster* created immediately after the event. All the data about the location, people, colors, shapes, etc. is exactly the same. This leaves the stimulus/response operating machinery of the subconscious no other choice but to activate the *bad cluster*. And with that, the connected negative physiological responses will automatically be carried out in the body.

We don't want to experience those feelings of pain, fear, and distress. We've managed to escape them in our heads; so, now we also want to escape from them physiologically. We won't even doubt the belief systems originating from it, just like Jenny did before she started applying *PMA*. We're clearly experiencing the activated feelings, which activate our *friend mechanism*, which will push us *away from pain* as far as possible by letting us conclude our beliefs are correct.

It sounds like we're dissociating every time a nasty memory pops up, one that's somehow related to a *bad cluster*. No, absolutely not. The *friend mechanism* has developed a much easier way to deal with this. Keep in mind that nasty memories like these are stored in a *cluster* which allows your conscious brain to deal with the moment. Whenever this *cluster* activates, the conscious brain will send a clear message to the subconscious that it doesn't want to see this nasty *cluster* again. Is it that simple? Yes, it is. The conscious brain will keep on repeating this message, loaded with rejection codes, from the moment the *cluster* pops up until the subconscious stops delivering its content. Remember, the subconscious brain is processing a million times more data than will ever reach the conscious. So, it doesn't really need this particular *cluster*.

The psychological expression for processing these particular *clusters* in this way is called *suppressed memories*.[10] Although the conscious doesn't want to see the content of the *cluster* anymore, it doesn't mean the subconscious won't use it in its comparison process. It will definitely use it. It doesn't have any choice, since it is a stimulus/response machine.

> *Your friend mechanism is a code-reading machine that protects you against pain and harm.*

Let's focus a little more on your *friend mechanism*. This is a code-reading machine that protects you against pain and harm. Something changes in that automatic process when you escape through your mind to another location. At a moment like that, your mind is disconnected from your body that is in distress.

The mind escapes to another level and is only aware of what happens there. Your *friend mechanism*, on the other hand, mainly reads the *physical* codes caused by biochemical

---

[10] For more details about suppressed memories, see Desirable Power.

interactions between your brain and the rest of your body. Your mind has disconnected itself from your body and you're only aware of things on an unusual level of consciousness.

Why an "unusual" level? Because we normally don't escape our bodies. We'll only do this when we feel as if we're unable to deal with the distress in our body and we're losing control. Existing without control is completely unnatural for us. We're not made for this type of distress, but we're not made to escape through our mind and flee to another realm of consciousness either. This creates a serious inner conflict in processing incoming sensory data. Now our subconscious receives data from the consciousness that has no connection anymore with the incoming data from the external world.

Our senses are not damaged during a *bad cluster* event. They're operating properly as always. It's our conscious brain that can't handle the situation, especially the panic feelings. It's our conscious brain that goes into *overload* and causes the

> *Our senses are not damaged during a bad cluster event. They're operating properly as always.*

mind to separate from the body, making its escape to a safer imaginary place in another realm. To be able to keep its concentration and stay in this imaginary escape, the consciousness starts blocking all sensory data that interferes or might disturb the process. Nevertheless, the senses are working normally, so all that consciously blocked sensory data *will* enter the brain and *will* be stored in the subconscious database. It will even be stored in exactly the same cells as correctly encoded *clusters*.

Although they are stored in the same place, there's a major difference between the *bad cluster* data and the *cluster* data. *All* data in a *cluster* carries correct *relative codes*. This means that every single piece of data has its own unique emotional importance. This is different in a *bad cluster* where all data have exactly the same *relative code* regardless of whether it's a color, sound, specific word, smell, taste, facial expression or anything else. All pieces of data have the same emotional load that was in our body at the moment the *bad cluster* happened. *All* of its data? Yes, all, but with the exception of a small group of data. There is *one* section in the *bad cluster* that's processed in a better, more normal way than the consciously rejected data.

> *There is one section in the bad cluster that's processed in a better, more normal way than the consciously rejected data.*

You remember reading about how to regain control during a *bad cluster* event? That's correct – we start focusing on a detail that will become our escape route. Our mind uses this as a bridge to the *holistic energetic world*. The detail is part of the *bad cluster*, but it's the only part that's processed in a more positive and normal way. It becomes the path out of the nasty event.

We're using this detail in *PMA* as a bridge to enter the content of the *bad cluster*. The discovery of your *bad cluster's* content is of great importance. Its powerful physiology empowers your *friend mechanism* in a negative way. Now, let's check the relationship between *bad clusters*, your *friend mechanism* and *your higher self*.

Your *friend mechanism* is universal. It is interwoven with your physical body as well as with the subconscious and conscious part of your brain. Its mechanism is even present in *your higher self* where it exists in its purest form. There are no inhibiting belief systems whatsoever to disturb the opinion of *your higher self* and, on that level, *bad clusters* have no effect on *your higher self* at all.

On the other hand, the *friend mechanism* in your physical body is *poisoned* by wrongly processed and incorrectly encoded *bad cluster* data. After a *bad cluster* is activated, its negative physiology manifests itself in your physical body and interrupts your normal functionality like a jamming signal. You're experiencing them as emotions and psychosomatic symptoms, and translating the physiological effects into belief systems. *This is how activated bad clusters finally become the power-source of inhibiting belief systems.*

Regardless of how powerful these feelings are, they do not affect the *intention* behind the *friend mechanism*. It's always staying true to its genetic program to keep you as far as possible from pain. Its intentions are always positive and protective. Although your *friend mechanism* is just a *mechanism*, the emotions and other physical signals it creates are very real and very personal to you. Those feelings shape a part of your character. They create *your* reality of the world.

Once you learn to know these feelings and fully accept them, you'll be surprised to see how they present themselves and what important companions they become on the road to success.

Chapter 8 – Your Energetic Realm

Bad cluster data will always be stored along with the unpleasant feelings that were present during that event. The one exception to this process is created by your escape actions at that specific time.

What do you do when distress level rises to the point where you feel you are losing control? You instinctively will find a way to *regain* that control. You will narrow your world down to a size that gives you back the control over your body, your emotions, and really, your whole self. How do you do that? By focusing on a *detail* in your surroundings. Your visual sense is the most powerful source of information; so, this detail will usually be something you look at. Whatever that is, it's got a color and a shape (like a painting, a person, an object, etc.), and you'll start focusing on that very intensely. It becomes your bridge to another level of awareness, a level in which your mind is in control again.

> You will narrow your world down to a size that gives you back the control.

Edward is in a car accident. Although he isn't wounded, he is in emotional shock because, for a moment, he has lost all control of his feelings. He's just staring at his hands on the steering wheel, blocking out all other incoming sensory data. He's slowly moving his fingers and finds some comfort in doing so. After doing this for a while, he begins to realize that he isn't hurt and returns to the full awareness of his whole body.

This whole event is stored unanalyzed and incorrectly encoded in a *bad cluster*. It is only the specific data of looking at his hands on the steering wheel that has reached his consciousness. This means that *all* other incoming sensory information was blocked at that brief moment and not correctly processed and encoded. The only data that is partially encoded is that little piece of information of his hands and fingers on the steering wheel he focused on. This part of the *bad cluster* data that felt safe for him at that time is stored as his *escape world*. Consequently, this part is now connected to fewer negative emotions (physiology) than all other *incorrectly* encoded *bad cluster* data. This small part also acts as a window into the *bad cluster* providing easier access to the remaining incorrectly encoded data. Follow? Once you've started tracing and transforming *bad clusters* that dictate your sabotaging beliefs, the way to success instantly opens up.

As mentioned earlier, the object or person of focus during our escape has a color and a shape. But what if you're unable to actually see during a *bad cluster* event? Then you'll have to use one of your other senses to create your *escape world*. But even if you do so, you'll still be able to use your visual sense in an *imaginary* way. By doing that, in your mind you'll still create some kind of *physical image* that has shape or color. Although you can't physically see with your eyes and although the "physical image" is only imaginary, for your mind it is real. We can all effortlessly move from one sense to the other in our brain cells.

Try and think of the *smell* of steak on a barbeque. Can you imagine the smell? Is it a big step for you to go from that *smell* to a *visual image* of a steak on a barbeque? For most people it's not even a step. They instantly see an image of a steak on a barbeque when trying to imagine its smell. So, you see, from a smell you effortlessly went to an image of a physical object.

Whatever you focus on during a *bad cluster* event, you will use as the *main* ingredient to build your own *escape world*. Understanding this process will create some insights into the origin of your *protectors*. What are protectors? During a *bad cluster* event you lose control over your emotions and body. That is unacceptable for your mind. Therefore, your mind will withdraw all its awareness from the body to focus intensely on that *escape world* that it created. That conscious experience will later on not merge with your huge subconscious database. It will create a small database of its own *escape world*. In other words, protectors are carriers of small parts of your life that hide their negative experiences from your everyday consciousness.

> *Protectors are the carriers of all your inhibiting belief systems; so, it's good to know all about them.*

Protectors are the carriers of all your inhibiting belief systems; so, it's good to know all about them. If you want to become rich (or achieve any other goal) you will definitely need to understand them and learn to cooperate with them. The creation and existence of your *protectors* are based on a familiar mechanism.

You're in the movie theater with some friends. They really like the movie they're watching, but you don't like it at all.

You're watching the screen and hearing the actors but your mind is at the beach. You smell the sea, hear the seagulls, and feel the sand. Your body's in the movie theatre but your mind is definitely not.

Naturally, you're not creating a *bad cluster* when your mind drifts off to a nice place like this. But essentially it's the same mechanism, except that in a *bad cluster* we go one huge step further. Although your mind was somewhere else when you were in the theatre, it was still connected to your body and had no intention of disconnecting. Escaping during a *bad cluster* situation is *not* based on boredom; on the contrary, fear or distress is causing your mind to *completely* escape your body. It feels as if your awareness is losing its connection with your body. In other words, you're losing control. Driven by panic, the mind is desperately searching for some kind of physical entity to hold on to. If there's no alternative it will take any other available object (or color, sound, shape, movement, etc.).

> *The mind is created in a way that it needs the connection with a physical body. But it also needs control.*

From the very first moment of our existence, our minds and bodies are connected. In a way, you could say they're one. The mind never needs to disconnect from the body in normal circumstances. But *bad clusters* are <u>not</u> formed during normal circumstances. The mind is created in a way that it needs the connection with a physical body. But it also needs control. So, when unusual things happen to us and the body starts acting uncontrollably, the mind will separate itself from the body. If our mind is forced to choose between its connection with the physical body or staying in control, it will automatically choose control. It's as if the mind needs a place to rest in order to regain its balance. Once this balance is established for the mind and the body, both can come together again.

These are two important aspects of the mind's behavior that need to be understood:

> *The mind is accustomed to being one with a physical body.*

> *During intense situations, the mind loses its conscious control of the body and its behavior.*

We have to consider that our mind represents our awareness. In a physical world our mind needs a physical body to express itself. Compare this to a composer creating a new melody in his mind. If he wants to express that music to others he needs his vocal cords or another physical body such as a musical instrument, to do so. This means if you dissociate to an *escape place*, the mind will merge with any suitable object that is available. This becomes the physical body that your mind will use to express itself. This also becomes the bridge between the separated mind and the physical body.

Even when the mind temporarily disconnects from your body and connects to another physical object, it's still *your* mind! Consequently, it still has awareness, *your* awareness. The only problem at these moments is that your awareness is not connected to its usual body. It feels more connected to this new object of focus. Imagine; it's almost as if your mind is living in two bodies at the same time.

According to the mind, staying in the other body feels safer than staying in the original body at that time. On the other hand, it also wants to *come home* again. To make that happen you have to convince that separated part of your mind that it is safe to do so. You have to convince it that its limited database that it has in the other body has created disturbing belief systems for the original body. You have to teach that part of your mind to understand that it does not need that object that it chose in panic to become its new home. The *protector* mind can simply come home to unite with the rest of your mind. In other words, you have to teach the *protector* how to *re-transform* into its original shape and location. This will create a powerful unity that can open up huge potential.

Whatever form you have dissociated to, is now not only part of a *bad cluster,* but has also become part of you, with all your feelings and thoughts at that very moment. You won't consciously remember these escape moments, but we all have many of them – all those moments in your childhood when you ran to your parents in a fright, or maybe the time a dog bit you, or when you had to go to a hospital or the dentist and got scared. All those moments are registered. Whenever you lost control, even for a split of a second, you created a *bad cluster.* Whenever something like this happened and you weren't able to physically escape by literally running away, you escaped through your mind. At these moments, your protectors were created in your mind to do exactly that – protect you.

> *You have to teach the protector how to re-transform into its original shape and location.*

Protectors are all very active and alive in your subconscious brain. They'll protect you wherever and however they can, based on the genetic program *away from pain*. Unfortunately, they can only protect you with what they know and their knowledge is very limited. They can only use the data that is stored in the *bad cluster* and the *cluster* that was created immediately after that event.

> Whenever you lost control, even for a split of a second, you created a bad cluster.

All their belief systems are based on *that* tiny amount of data. What kind of data is that? It's the data of the *escape world* that you created during the *bad cluster* event. It contains the ingredients you were concentrating on and that you created in your *escape world*. This created the only tools it has available to protect you. So, whatever belief systems were created during and after the *bad cluster* will now be used in a very powerful way.

How do these *bad clusters* relate to the belief systems and feelings we created in our *escape world?* How do we establish contact with these hidden feelings? And maybe even more important, how do we deal with all this now in order to create the most positive outcome for our future? We'll discuss the technique for this later on in greater detail but, for now, let's look at the example of Susan and how she was able to find answers in applying the *PMA technique.*

Susan was a normal, healthy three-year-old. She was running around in the living room holding on to her teddy bear, when she hit a small table. An antique vase that her father had inherited from his grandmother tilted and fell to the floor, smashing into a thousand pieces. Her father became furious. He struck Susan in the face screaming: *"Look what you did! This priceless vase, you've ruined it! I can never buy a vase like this again! It's all your fault! It's been in our family for four generations and now it's gone. Now I can't pass it on to you. Ah, you don't deserve it anyway!"* He went on and on, Susan felt like he was never going to stop. She was terrified and couldn't handle the situation, and, eventually, lost control. *"Go to your room! I never want to see you again!"* As if in a trance, she went to her room and lay down on the bed.

During that whole event, she regained control by focusing on the brown teddy bear she was holding in her arms. She started talking to it in her mind. Now she was totally in her *energetic realm* with her teddy bear and heard or felt nothing else.

What did Susan store in her subconscious? All the sensory data of her father shouting at her was stored in a *bad cluster*. Every piece of data was loaded with the scary feelings of that time. Finally, though, her father calmed down and Susan felt safe enough to return from her *escape place* to her body. Her father was still upset and kept talking about the value of that priceless vase. Susan stored the uncontrollable part of the event in a *bad cluster* and the later part of it when she was alone with her teddy bear in her bedroom, in a regular *cluster*.

As we know by now, *bad clusters* cannot spontaneously be approached by the conscious brain. The small *window* that allows us to peek inside of the *bad cluster* is that *specific detail* we focused on when we minimized our world to a controllable size. How are we going to do this? What did we do with the detail after we used it?

This is how Susan's teddy bear became the face of one of her *protectors*. A *protector* is not another person inside of you. It's *you* at a *specific place*, at a *specific time* in your life. The data of that place and time is, so to speak, stored at a separate partition of your subconscious hard drive. *Protectors* are always born during panic, pain and distress. We don't like these feelings and therefore our *friend mechanism* will suppress as much data as possible that could connect to these *protectors*. The only data that the *friend mechanism* will not suppress are the belief systems and behavior patterns of the *protectors*, because they create a feeling of comfort. Even if you consciously have no awareness of their presence, subconsciously they are always there to help and protect you.

> A protector is not another person inside of you. It's you at a specific place, at a specific time in your life.

They will also help you to become rich because those *protectors* possess a lot of wisdom and knowledge. They're much easier to approach and much more cooperative than you might think. They're not simply mechanisms like your *friend mechanism*. The data that created them is a part of you. This isn't the right place to explain the how's and why's, but what is important to understand is that these *protectors*, these feelings, have been suppressed for a long time and they want to be heard. They have protected you over and over again and have all the right in the world to be heard! And, you know what? They're ready to communicate with you, but they can only help you if you listen to them. The question is: Are you able and ready to do that? Are you ready to get the success in life you deserve?

When I first encountered this phenomenon, I thought: *"Come on, Jacob, you're an intelligent, rational thinking guy. You can't really believe you have "protectors" in your body that have color and shape and can even talk to you. You want me to believe that a rational person like me has to contact "protectors" inside of me and that I have to start a conversation with a thing!?"*

Then, I thought, *"But so far, being a rational, intellectual person has not delivered any helpful answers in transforming any of my sabotaging beliefs. What can I lose in trying this out?"*

> *It's all about the willingness to accept unusual possibilities.*

It also dawned on me that there wasn't any risk involved. On the contrary, the risk was in NOT trying this out. Actually, I felt this was going to be kind of fun. I concluded that it's all about the willingness to accept unusual possibilities. Some people might think this weird or unrealistic, but the fact is that none of those rational "know-it-all's" have any effective answers to the question: *"How can I transform inhibiting belief systems that have been sabotaging me in so many aspects in life?"*

I made the decision to try this technique and you won't believe the amount of enlightening answers I have gotten ever since. I am still amazed every day how many financial opportunities are presented to me since I transformed my beliefs.

We'll discuss the details of the technique in the next chapters but let's review Susan's story and see how she used the *PMA technique* to her advantage.

> Susan is now thirty-two years old and has had a strong desire to become wealthy for years now. Although she did everything in her power to make it work, it hasn't happened so far. But once she understood the existence of her *higher self* and the power of *bad clusters*, everything starts to change. She finally begins to understand that whenever she has an opportunity to make a lot of money, she sabotages herself. She simply doesn't or can't hear or see the opportunity. She just seems to have a total lack of judgment.

> Applying *PMA*, Susan goes back in her memory to relive the moments when she started sabotaging herself. After she finds the exact moment and details of sabotaging, she feels a strong resistance to continue the process. She asks herself: *"What color does this resistance have?"* Instantly she knows. It is brown. *"What shape does it have?"* Right away she sees the image of a teddy bear. One of her *protectors* has immediately revealed himself to her.

> Susan invites the *protector* into her *safe place* together with her *higher self*. She asks the teddy bear what it wants to achieve by giving her this inhibiting feeling and lack of judgment. The answer is: *"Stopping you from focusing on wealth and money."* She asks: *"I know you want to protect*

me and you mean well, so what is it that you ultimately want to achieve with that?" "To protect you from pain," is the answer. She continues: *"Can you help me understand why you experience wealth as painful?"* Her *protector* replies: *"Wealth means having valuable possessions. Valuables are always causing pain because they break. Wealth means you'll be isolated and lonely. The ones you love will abandon you."*

Susan instantly recognizes the feelings; her *protector* hasn't told her anything new. She starts to understand that she intuitively knows the feeling but that she isn't consciously aware of its origin or the connected belief systems. She has no idea how or where her inhibiting belief systems were made by this *protector*. She isn't able to make the logical connections to the broken vase because that event was hidden in a *bad cluster* and the aftermath in a *suppressed cluster*. But somehow the *protector*'s feelings and the belief systems feel very familiar.

Using the *PMA technique*, Susan continues the discussion with her *protector*:

"I know you want the best for me, but would you be willing to change your approach and help me develop other feelings about wealth and money?" The *protector* responds: *"My beliefs have worked perfectly so far, why should I change them?" "I'm sure you created these belief systems to protect me at the time, but now they're creating a lot of damage for you and me. That's why I want to ask you if you'd be willing to help me and transform your*

power in a way that we'll both benefit? Are you willing to do that?" Susan instantly feels her *protector* is willing to cooperate.

In the beginning, while you're getting used to the process, you might have actual conversations with *your higher self* and your *protectors*. Once you regularly apply the process, you'll notice that words won't always be necessary. You'll experience the presence of *your higher self* and your *protectors* and you will simply *know* and *feel* their answers without one word spoken. Keep in mind that energy is a fast-moving thing and so is your subconscious. All these communications take place in the *energetic realm*. As stated before, your subconscious processes about a million times more data per second than your conscious brain can handle.

> *Once you regularly apply the process, you'll notice that words won't always be necessary. You will simply know and feel their answers without one word spoken.*

Your conscious awareness and your *protectors* have already communicated with you when they gave you these gut feelings that told you, when you had to make a decision in life, that your decisions and actions were right or wrong. These feelings can pop up at any given moment when decisions or choices need to be made. Most of the time, such signals did not use words but use a simple feeling. Are you beginning to realize all the perks the *PMA* technique can give you? You have the power to open an entire world for yourself. Let's return to Susan and see how she continues.

Susan asks her *protector:*

> *"How old was I when you started helping me?"* Instantly the answer comes: *"Three years old."* From that point on, Susan continues on her own by asking herself: *"Where am I at this time? Am I somewhere inside or outside?"* Instantly, a picture of the living room pops up. *"Am I alone there?"* Immediately she sees her father there. *"What is happening there?"* She sees the very moment that she breaks the very expensive vase, the one her father inherited from his grandmother.

Susan remembers and although she's heard the story from her parents many times, she never had a clear image of the event until now. Then comes the emotions that she felt when she was young. She knows she was on the right track when she asks herself:

> *"What is the most painful moment there?"* The reactions of her body indicates it was when her father was screaming and hitting her. Now she goes for the most painful *detail.* She starts reliving the moment and instantly she feels the detail. It is clearly the angry look in her father's eyes. His look caused a feeling of rejection, fear, and panic, feelings that she is reliving at this moment.

All kinds of memories start flying through her head. She's back in the living room at the age of three, walking up the stairs into her bedroom, and holding her teddy tightly to her chest. She's lying in bed and feeling horribly sad and lonely. She's afraid her father will stay angry with her for the rest of her life.

It all comes back to her in a flash. The words of her father, for instance: *"Look at what you did! This priceless vase, you've ruined it! I can never buy a vase like this again! It's all your fault!"*... and on, and on.

Susan understands how this event had led to her belief systems and how she has created a *protector*, in this case a teddy bear, when she was three years old. She also understands why the teddy bear became so very important to her at that point. It was just a carrier she had used to connect her feelings to. She now understands the origin of her negative beliefs about wealth: *"Wealth means having valuable possessions. Valuables are always causing pain because they break. Wealth means you'll be isolated and lonely. The ones you love will abandon you."*

In a split a second, her brain made all these connections and all her negative feelings disappeared.[11] What is the result for Susan? She benefits in many ways. She suddenly understands her beliefs and feelings about money and wealth. She becomes totally aware of how her subconscious comparison material created hidden belief systems and why she was not even aware of them before *PMA*. Now she is able to change them into powerful motivating ones. She can also get rid of the horrible feelings of loneliness she had been suffering from for so many years. Her relationship with her father improves because her long existing unexplainable feelings of fear and distance disappeared. And last but not least, her financial status starts growing steadily. After her *protector* changes its inhibiting powers into a driving force to gain wealth, it reunites itself

---

[11] Study Desirable Power to see why these feelings disappear and do not return.

with Susan's subconscious database. In psychology this process is called *integration*.

Is it always this easy? As for the *PMA* process, yes, it is. The only one capable of making it difficult is <u>*you*</u>, by doubting what you already know, deep inside, for so long. You just have to make the decision to listen. Some people might have just one single *bad cluster* interfering with their desire to become rich. Others might have several of these *bad cluster* events causing their inhibiting belief systems. Some might feel the whole *protector* explanation is more metaphoric than reality, while others instantly feel and know what it's all about and experience it realistically!

> *Is it always this easy? As for the PMA process, yes, it is. The only one capable of making it difficult is <u>you</u>,*

To create powerful results with the *PMA technique*, it is not important if you believe the explanations are true or not, as long as you apply the technique. After a while, you will discover automatically how true the explanations are. Anyone who applies the *PMA* technique and explores its effects in his personal life will have sensational, instant, and long lasting results.

We've all experienced losing our objectivity when a problem seems too big. Just realize what great insight we've already gained here, and we haven't even started the real process yet! Isn't it almost magical that we can just step out of ourselves and our disturbed feelings? You just have to step into this *energetic realm.* You'll be surprised at how fast things in your life will change.

Chapter 9 — Combining Your Forces

It's time now to summarize all of this new knowledge and make you understand why you need all the information I provided. What do we have so far?

Clusters:
Correctly coded data of events (memories), good and bad, with a tolerable degree of emotions.

Bad Clusters:
Incorrectly encoded data of panic-events in which you've lost control. Every single piece of data in it is loaded with negative feelings that you experienced in the past. Once transformed, huge amounts of energy will be set free for positive use.

Friend Mechanism:
Genetic stimulus/response code-reading mechanism that's programmed to keep you *away from pain,* as far as possible.

Belief Systems:
Beliefs about every aspect in life, good and bad. Everything you do is based on your belief systems. More than 75% of your belief systems originate from *bad cluster* material, inhibiting and sabotaging you.

Your Higher Self:
Your unlimited potential. All you know, all you are, all your hidden potentials. You have unlimited access to *your higher*

self in the energetic world where your mind operates.

Your Protectors: Behavioral patterns in a *bad cluster* event that created your *escape world*. The awareness of their existence is suppressed. They're the source behind your inhibiting belief systems.

These six components will provide you with *all* you need to reach your full potential and get rich, stay rich, and enjoy your wealth. In time, you'll even discover these ingredients are also the road to much, much more than just financial wealth. But those are other topics for other books. How are we going to work with these six components?

The first step is to realize they represent *all* your potential in *all* areas of your life. They were always there; they were just hidden from your conscious brain. You weren't aware of their endless capacities, so, you didn't consult them. Now, this will change.

Let's start and focus on combining our forces and cooperating with them to reach the highest level of success. The following steps will show you how to use the six components, followed by the transformation of your sabotaging and inhibiting belief systems into proactive energy generators. The steps can be used in any aspect of your daily life. They apply to any question you have, any problem that arises, any decision you have to make, or any actions you are planning to take. You can share the bad stuff with *your higher self* and your *protectors* but you can also share all the fun stuff.

Step 1 – Realization of your higher self

Realize that *your higher self* <u>always</u> wants the best for you, is <u>always</u> there for you, and is an endless source of answers, ideas, advice and whatever other support you need. Never exclude *your higher self* from whatever you undertake in your life. *Your higher self* is always there as your powerful source and advisor in all of the following steps. Ask *your higher self* frequently to support and advise you.

Step 2 – Realization of your protectors

Realize that your *protectors* <u>always</u> want to help and protect you and that they have no intention of harming you. However, your *protectors* are limited to the very small database they created during the *bad cluster* event when they became active. They have the power of a giant but the judgment of a child. You have to help them understand that their interference saved you in the past, but is limiting and even harming you today. You've got all the reasons in the world to be grateful to them for what they've done for you. But from today on, you have to educate them and give them access to your total database. They're <u>always</u> cooperative and as your reliable companions, they really want only the best for you.

Step 3 – Learn to know the appearances of your protectors

Bad cluster events can occur in many places and in many situations. Therefore, you'll never know the ingredients you've used to create your *escape world*. If you've got many *bad clusters*, your *protectors* will have many different colors, shapes, and ages. Some of them might even be present in several *bad clusters*. Get to know them really well.

Step 4 – Open and honest communication

Invite your *protectors* into your *safe place*. Get comfortable, sit in an easy chair, and invite every one of them to speak up about their issues and how they're trying to help you in their unique way. Remember, they're acting like *protectors*. They have no intention of harming or inhibiting you in any way. The fact that they are sabotaging you now is purely due to a current lack of knowledge and insight. Some of them work closely together with other *protectors*. In very complicated cases, you might even have *protectors* that protect other (mostly younger) *protectors*. If you discover there's more than one *protector* associated with a specific topic, then invite them *all* to *your safe place* and communicate with them *all*. Never try to deceive them. Realize that *your higher self* is always present and that he knows every single aspect about you, even your deepest thoughts, feelings, wishes and desires.

Step 5 – Cooperate with your higher self and your protectors

Don't ever hesitate to invite one or more of your *protectors* into your *safe place* to communicate with you and *your higher self*. All your *protectors* want to be heard. Their intention is always to help and protect you. If you show them that they are doing this inadequately, they will be more than willing to find new ways to protect and help you.

Step 6 – Discover the true intentions of your protectors

Your *protectors* are always the source behind feelings that you experience as inhibiting, upsetting and/or sabotaging. If these feelings (disturbed physiology) exist for a longer period of time they can even cause emotional and physical diseases.[12] As soon as you're in contact with one of your *protectors*, ask him: *"What do you want? What's the purpose of the feelings you've created in my body?"* Keep asking until you receive a satisfying answer.

When asked, *"what do you want,"* your *protector* might, for instance, reply with: *"I want to make you tired."* You could ask: *"Why?"* Your *protector* could answer: *"To slow you down."* To your question of why you have to slow down, your *protector* might answer: *"If you don't slow down, you'll exhaust all your reserves and get sick or die."* Now you know your *protector* has told you the purpose of his actions.

Step 7 – Always seek advice from your higher self

Sometimes, it might seem like you can't find the correct manifestations of a *protector* or you don't know how to continue and ask the right questions to get the information you need. Seek the advice of *your higher self* whenever you get stuck.

---

[12] See Desirable Power

Step 8 – Discuss the transformation and growth of protectors

You, *your higher self,* and your *protectors,* have to create a new task together for the *protectors.* They want to be the source of your most effective protection, happiness, and health and will reroute their enormous energy to support you fully. To accomplish that, you have to devise a plan and mutual agreement on how to do that.

Step 9 – Find the origin of your protectors

The next step is to discover when and where your *protectors* came to life. Ask: *"How old were we when you first started helping me?"* When your *protector* started helping you, it might not know where you were and what happened because it escaped to its own little world. So, from this point on, continue by asking yourself the following questions: *"Where am I? Am I somewhere inside or outside? Is it cold or warm there? (If inside) Is it a large or a small room? Am I alone or are there others with me? What do I see there? What is happening there?"*

Step 10 – Transform bad clusters into positive energy

When you discover where and when your *protector* was created, you gain your first insight into the corresponding *bad cluster.* This isn't the whole content of the *bad cluster* but you've now found a *window* that allows you to glance at its content. You're usually in the *cluster* now that was created right after the *bad cluster.* This particular *cluster* contains lots of information about the *event* you're searching for. Now, keep on following the easy *PMA* protocol, as described in the next paragraphs, until the whole content of the *bad cluster* presents itself.

When you've found the *cluster* right after the *event*, isolate the scariest _moment_ in that situation. When you have this *moment*, just focus on it and isolate the most powerful _detail_ in it. How do you know you've found the right *moment* and *detail*? Your body will instantly tell you. How? By increasing the negative feelings you're experiencing. Your feelings are your reliable guide in this simple *PMA* procedure:

Event – Moment – Detail – Feeling

Once you have the detail and become aware of your feelings, it's important that you don't try to *remember* or *think* about it. Just focus on the _detail_ and the feelings until a new picture _spontaneously_ pops up. It's the same mechanism that you're using when daydreaming. Don't think, don't conclude, and don't try to remember; just *wait*.

Once this next spontaneous picture pops up, you've found your next _event_. Now just repeat the same *PMA* procedure:

Event – Moment – Detail – Feeling

Keep doing this until the next spontaneous picture pops up. Keep repeating the procedure until you feel that your feelings are really intensifying. Now you're almost there. The next mental image that pops up is usually the *bad cluster*. How do you know you've found it? You feel it immediately. The mega-speed of your subconscious connecting process makes all the tension, fear, or any other negative feelings you were experiencing, disappear in seconds. This *bad cluster* will never bother you again because it has permanently been transformed into a motivating positive energy.

The great thing about it is you don't have to do this transformation by yourself. *Your higher self* and your *protectors* are always there to support you. Never be shy to ask for their support.

Chapter 10 – The Source of Resistance

Will the procedure always unfold this easily or can you expect resistance? If you feel any form of resistance, then *you* are the source of that! *Your higher self* and your *protectors* are always committed to help you. Resistance is always the result of activated comparison material. This follows the exact same pattern as we've discussed before. As soon as your *friend mechanism* reads a high *relative code* (indicating negative emotions) it will automatically push it as far away from your awareness as possible, following the genetic program *away from pain.*

> *Whenever you feel resistance, regardless about what issue, the first thing you have to do is make a decision!*

Whenever you feel resistance, regardless about what issue, the first thing you have to do is make a decision! It's all about your decisions. You're always in charge of your decisions. They're not based on rational reasons but always on your emotions. To make the right decision, you need emotional leverage. Desire is a powerful decision-maker. It will help you in asking yourself the following questions:

> ➢ *How strong is your desire to transform your negative belief systems into proactive energy?*

> ➢ *How strong is your desire to get rich?*

> ➢ *How strong is your desire to feel happy?*

> ➢ *How strong is your desire to have a wonderful relationship?*

> ➤ *How strong is your desire to be energetic and healthy?*

> ➤ *How strong is your desire to unfold your full potentials?*

Is there anything wrong with the desires mentioned above? Will the fulfillment of these desires hurt or damage you or anybody else? Is their fulfillment against any law? Do they interfere with anybody's freedom or rights? No? Well then, what's the logic of having inhibiting belief systems against the fulfillment of any of them? A resistance like that would definitely not serve you.

Whenever resistance arises, *protectors* are involved. But it's completely irrelevant to your *friend mechanism* whether the negative feelings are coming from *bad clusters*, *protectors* or any other source. Although it cannot suppress the feelings, it will read the attached negative *relative codes* and automatically pushes the data as far away from your awareness as possible.

Before you had any knowledge about *PMA*, you had no conscious awareness of *bad clusters*, your *friend mechanism*, your higher self or your protectors. So, you also didn't know about the hidden source of resistance created by *bad clusters* and how to deal with them in a beneficial way. But from now on, whenever inhibiting and sabotaging belief systems pop up and generate resistance you know you're dealing with one of your

> *Whenever inhibiting and sabotaging belief systems pop up and generate resistance you know you're dealing with one of your protectors.*

protectors. A *protector* inspires inhibiting belief systems because it somehow experienced that owning, using, keeping or enjoying money is bad for you. The protector is totally convinced that you have to stay away from money, wealth or any other thing related to prosperity. It will amaze you time and again to discover how twistedly our brains stored *bad cluster* information and how that affects your current decisions and actions. Through *PMA* you'll be able to trace the cause behind their driving forces and transform their energy into power that serves you.

Whenever you feel resistance coming from your *protectors,* you can choose to communicate with them or not. Pushing the feelings of resistance away will only rob you from the opportunity of transforming them. To win your *protectors* over to a positive transformation of their belief systems you have to get in conscious contact with them and their origin. Then you will understand them in their proper and positive context and understand why they act as they do and why they believe their actions serve and protect you. *Protectors,* along with their thoughts and feelings, are a part of you. They don't just appear without cause. They're produced by *your* brain, *your* mind, *your* body. Therefore, you have to be careful how you approach these feelings of resistance.

Resistance is always a feeling, an emotion. Each issue or topic will activate its own set of belief systems, which will generate their own level of specific physical symptoms of resistance. To get in contact with your *protectors* just follow the procedure as explained in Chapters 5, 6, and 8.

As soon as a specific feeling of resistance comes up, start with asking *your higher self* for the right cause of action. Ask him how he perceives the issue of your resistance. Would he advise you to find the hidden cause and reason for your resistance? Ask him if it would serve you to ignore the feeling and to keep holding on to your inhibiting belief systems? Would it help you to grow towards a higher level in life if the resistance would no longer control you?

Once you and *your higher self* are in agreement that it would definitely serve you if the resistance would change into a motivational energy, you can continue on to the next step. *Your higher self* will always tell you that illogical resistance will never serve you. Transforming inhibiting belief systems

> *Your higher self will always tell you that illogical resistance will never serve you.*

into motivating ones, though, will open up a huge source of opportunities.

Bottom-line is: *What is your decision?* You're the only one that can make the decision of transforming your sabotaging belief systems into empowering ones. Nobody can force you to do so and no one else can move you towards luck, happiness and wealth other than yourself. It all comes down to how great *your* desire is to achieve those things to the highest possible level.

Now that you understand how powerful *bad clusters* are and how they can sabotage you in, for instance, your attempt to become rich, you'll probably agree with me that you don't need *bad clusters* to be happy. You'll want to stop them empowering negative belief systems that sabotage your financial abilities ASAP. You'll want to merge with *all* your *protectors* and their enormous power to reach your fullest potential in unity.

Understanding the existence and power of *bad clusters* is one thing, but transforming their negative power into large amounts of positive energy is another. The *PMA technique* enables you to achieve all this and it's easy to apply. Your *protectors* aren't some kind of mysterious power inside or outside your body that stops you. You have created them and suppressed the awareness of their existence afterwards. It all comes down to *your decision* to communicate with them and allow them to show you the way.

> *PMA will help you discover that you have many hidden skills and potentials.*

Just remember that this powerful genetic force *away from pain* always drives your friend mechanism. It will always follow its genetic program and, therefore, will always lead you *away from pain* as quickly as possible. Keep in mind that *PMA* is such an easy procedure to learn, but it's only effective if you take your *friend mechanism* into consideration and if you fully cooperate with *your higher self* and your *protectors*. They will help you discover that you have many hidden skills and potentials. Just imagine what this could mean for your future, for your relationships, your wealth and your career!

You might think: *"Can I do this all by myself?"* Yes, you can. It just depends on how honest you are with yourself. It basically comes down to this question: *How much do you respect and love yourself?* Unhappy people usually live a lie. They keep conditioning themselves with their inhibiting belief systems and keep on sabotaging their own health, wealth and happiness. In order to transform the negative physiology of your own *bad clusters* into positive energy, it's very important to learn and allow yourself to look at *anything* your *protectors* show you during this *PMA* procedure.

Some people tell us they find it difficult to trust the memories that spontaneously pop up. What they actually mean is that they have a hard time believing these memories are true. They tend to say: *"But how do I know I didn't make them up?"* The great thing is: It's entirely irrelevant to the transformation process whether the memories are true or not. It's all about the amount of negative feelings attached to the memories. As soon as you consciously become aware of the *bad cluster* images, their negative symptoms (physiology) will flow away in a matter of seconds. This will have an instant positive effect on your energy and will transform your inhibiting beliefs, regardless whether you want to believe in the authenticity of the memories or not.

> *It's entirely irrelevant to the transformation process whether the memories are true or not. It's all about the amount of negative feelings attached to the memories.*

At the very moment that you become consciously aware of the memories, your subconscious starts to process the data in them at mega speed. A million times faster than your conscious brain, it will connect the negative data of the *bad cluster* to thousands and thousands of other pieces of data, loaded with positive energy. Now every piece of data is properly processed and correctly encoded. It will never bother you again.

The *PMA technique* is very easy and straightforward: Always start with an _event_ that made you feel uncomfortable or created an unpleasant feeling of resistance with regards to money or business issues. Just go back to any of the events that come to mind. Now *relive* that event with all your senses. *Be there again.* In doing so, your body will exactly tell you the most uncomfortable _moment_ and _detail_. You won't discover them by thinking or using your conscious memory. You can only find them by reliving that wrongly stored specific event.

It's of great importance to realize that, so far, reasoning and a rational approach have *never* provided any insight into your sabotaging mechanisms. The *PMA technique* as described in this book takes place on another level of awareness. To achieve the highest results you have to allow *your higher self* and your *protectors* to lead you

> *Your body will exactly tell you the most uncomfortable moment and detail.*

without any rational interference! To put it as plainly as possible: After your feelings have shown you the _moment_ followed by the _detail_, you do _nothing_! Just focus on the particular _detail_ and _allow the feelings to intensify_ without fighting or suppressing them.

Remember that your subconscious database has gathered an abundance of comparison material throughout your life and that your subconscious brain is a stimulus/response machine, it will always automatically process incoming data. In this case, the data is coming from inside because your conscious brain keeps focusing on *one detail*. The conscious brain is not only focusing on that one detail but it's also allowing all the feelings (*relative code*) that are connected to that detail. In normal circumstances, the *friend mechanism* will read these negative *relative codes* and push them aside to make room for more positive *relative codes*. But this time the conscious brain is very persistent. Along with focusing on the detail, it also very determined to become aware of its connected negative feelings. This persistent attitude forces the subconscious to deliver the necessary comparison material. If you'll allow your subconscious to deliver this comparison material without rational interference, you'll be surprised at what you'll discover about the source of your inhibiting belief systems and your hidden potential.

> *If you'll allow your subconscious to deliver all its comparison material without rational interference, you'll be surprised at what you'll discover.*

What do you do after another memory pops up? Just follow the same procedure: Now this other memory is your new *event*. Now go and find the *moment* in that event, followed by the discovery of the *detail* in that moment. Focus on the *detail* again and allow your *feelings* to come up. To avoid disturbing the process during the procedure you will have to:

Relive

Reliving means that you:

See – Feel – Hear – Taste – Smell

In your mind, you're at the same location again with all of your senses. *Reliving* is not the same as just *remembering* an event. You *have* to be there again, but this time just in your mind while your body is now in a safe place. Keep in mind that all the data of a *bad cluster* is stored in your subconscious brain. It cannot logically be remembered. It doesn't matter how hard you try, you cannot *rationally* discover the content of a *bad cluster*!

> *You have to put the rational approach on hold. Just watch and experience the unfolding of the mental pictures without any interruption.*

The data is in the subconscious and you can only find it through a specific approach. In order to achieve fast and optimal results, you have to put the rational approach on hold. Just watch and experience the unfolding of the mental pictures without any interruption. To be able to accomplish this, during the *PMA procedure* you:

➤ *Don't think*

➤ *Don't reason*

➤ *Don't argue*

➤ *Don't summarize*

➤ *Don't describe why*

➤ *Don't control the direction*

All these tasks are rational processes. As soon as you've reached the contents of a *bad cluster*, you'll start to understand many incidents in your life when you felt activated or blocked in your efforts and behavior but didn't know why. You'll also understand all the inhibiting belief systems you created based on those inexplicable feelings. Always realize this:

> ➤ *Whatever it is that created a bad cluster in your past, it did not kill you!*

> ➤ *Reliving doesn't mean you have to experience the entire magnitude of the panic of the original event. It'll be there for a split of a second and then it'll be gone forever to make place for positive peaceful energy.*

> ➤ *Keep in mind that your friend mechanism will automatically try to stop you. It might even come up with unrealistic pictures. Don't ignore those pictures and invite the feelings they carry to come up!*

> ➤ *Remember: You're not looking for the objective truth in this procedure. You're looking for mental pictures that you couldn't consciously remember and that are loaded with negative physiology.*

What will surprise you most is discovering how many of your belief systems, preferences, habits and decisions are based upon *bad clusters*. The same goes for unexplainable fears and emotional blockages. The more you trace and transform these things, the more mental energy will be released. Your learning capabilities and memory will also improve, and your inhibiting and sabotaging belief systems will disappear forever. So, in summarizing all this:

> *Using the PMA process and finding bad clusters means you have to <u>relive.</u>*

> *Reliving means: just moving from one mental picture to the next.*

> *<u>Don't</u> think, reason, or rationalize about the mental pictures that pop up.*

> *Just experience whatever your subconscious offers you spontaneously.*

> *Hear, smell, see, feel (touch) and taste.*

> *Allow all <u>spontaneous</u> emotions and mental pictures to present themselves, and do not suppress them!*

It's the easiest thing; it's all automatic if you don't block it! You'll know exactly when you've arrived at the *bad cluster*. Although you're consciously becoming aware of the images for the first time, they'll create a feeling that you'll instantly recognize. Even when years have passed after the real event, the data will now be processed and correctly encoded as a normal *cluster*. The negative physiology will instantly leave your body and never return. You'll experience a great relief that will positively affect you in all the ways we've discussed. The related inhibiting belief systems will melt away like snow for the sun. Let us now start transforming your sabotaging belief systems about money and wealth.

Chapter 11 – Transforming Your Belief Systems

To achieve more wealth than you have right now, your inhibited belief systems towards money and wealth have to be transformed. If they don't change, your decisions, actions, and behaviors won't change and you'll receive what you've always received.

In order to determine which belief systems to transform, you need to identify and know them. Once you know your inhibiting belief systems you'll be able to choose and transform them into motivating ones. In the context of this book, we'll focus exclusively on inhibiting belief systems that are related to money and wealth.

Literally *everything* we decide and do is based on our belief systems. We have many beliefs that serve us very well; we don't have to worry about them. Transforming belief systems is all about those beliefs that *don't* serve you well. They only inhibit and sabotage you. There are two misleading aspects here:

1. *Your superficial belief systems aren't always what you really believe deep down inside.*

2. *Your most powerful inhibiting belief systems don't feel like negative beliefs to you at all. On the contrary, they feel very good to you.*

You might think that what you easily express as being your belief systems (*surface*) are also your *real* beliefs on a deeper level. To verify this, just ask *your higher self.* We all have a tendency to get shaky here, so take your time with this process. Some beliefs are so strong and feel so right to us that we don't really wait for this validation. Instead, we already provide the answer before our *higher self* even has the chance to speak.

We all have belief systems that we hold on to with all our power and that we defend to the very end. Some of those beliefs deserve this kind of devotion, but others don't. Those belief systems that usually don't have a positive outcome for us are the ones we have to discover and transform. Once again, ask *your higher self*. You'll instantly know and feel the right answer to the question.

Another criterion in helping you in discover whether a belief system is driven by an ordinary *cluster* or a *bad cluster* is your conscious memory of its roots. Regardless of which belief system we're talking about, it's always good to trace the origin. If the belief stems from ordinary *clusters*, you'll have no trouble backtracking. If you're having difficulty, then there's a strong chance the origins are from a *bad cluster*. And again, always ask *your higher self* for input.

Now we'll go ahead and use all the insights and knowledge we've gathered so far in our *belief system transformation process*. There are four important areas related to money and wealth:

❖ *Making money*

❖ *Using money*

❖ *Keeping money*

❖ *Enjoying money*

In Chapters 13 to 16, you'll find many statements leading to your belief systems about specific issues. The four areas stated in these chapters are <u>not</u> separated by time. They are aspects about money and wealth that play a role at the same time. From the start, your belief systems about each one of them play an important role. The list covers the majority of all issues that people have with money and wealth. Let's see how to use these statements and find our inhibiting beliefs. We'll use the following statement as an example:

My need for an abundant amount of money

1☐ 2☐ 3☐ 4☐ 5☐ 6☐ 7☐ 8☐ 9☐ 10☐

Assume you're feeling resistance to this particular statement. Let's say your level of comfort with this statement is a 3. Ask yourself: *Why is it a 3 and not a 10?* Your belief systems will tell you exactly *why* you feel that it's a *3* and not a *10*. The reasons and arguments you'll come up with to explain *why* you're feeling so uncomfortable with this statement, represent your belief systems.

You might have a powerful belief system that says: *"I don't need money to be happy!"* In itself correct, but be honest, isn't having an abundance of wealth a lot of fun? You might respond: *"Money doesn't grow on trees; it's a struggle earning it. Besides, money makes you corrupt."* Would you agree that with beliefs like these, it's very difficult to evoke a drive towards making, using, keeping and enjoying an abundance of money and wealth? Will these kinds of beliefs program you for wealth or will they sabotage you in becoming rich? Whatever you believe determines your behavior and level of success.

After you've filled in your level of comfort with a statement, your belief systems usually pop right up; especially the positive ones. They originate from ordinary *clusters* and you'll have no resistance to them. These are not the ones we want to transform. The ones we want to run through the *PMA transformation process* are the negative ones – those that inhibit and sabotage you. They're the ones that caused the lower number that you assigned to the statement.

Some of the statements activate spontaneous resistance. These are exactly the statements you look for. In that case, your belief systems might hesitate to pop up. If so, ask yourself the following questions:

> ➤ *Is the figure I gave myself on this statement realistic?*

> ➤ *Why do I believe it's realistic?*

> ➤ *Why do I believe I'm at this level of comfort?*

> ➤ *Is this my desired level?*

> ➤ *If not, what belief systems are stopping me from getting where I want to be?*

> ➤ *What personal belief system forms the basis for my reaction to this particular statement?*

> ➤ *Am I satisfied with my score?*

> ➤ *Would I like to change this belief system?*

> ➤ *If the answer is no, why not?*

> ➤ *If the answer is yes, what is stopping me from making the necessary changes?*

If you don't know the answers to these questions right off, ask *your higher self* to assist you. All these questions lead to your belief systems. Whatever beliefs already popped up, take the time to write them down and, of course, continue reading the book. Go back when you've finished and start filling in your personal levels of comfort with each of the statements in chapter 13-16. Then, as soon as you've found a statement that doesn't feel comfortable, *don't continue* on to the next statement until after you've finished the process of transforming that particular belief system.

After you've found a statement that activates negative beliefs, write them down. Now, imagine being able to get rid of each of these beliefs and replacing them with belief systems that would create an entirely different response and behavior. You have to change them in a way that they'd really serve you well. Be aware of the fact that these new beliefs are not just words. You'll continue to *stick to them* in every future event that would otherwise have stirred up the old beliefs. Think of what the next issue could be where these new beliefs could apply. Make this as realistic as possible.

Now pay attention to your feelings. If your old inhibiting beliefs originate from ordinary *clusters* you'll feel totally fine with your new beliefs and you'll be happy to apply them. However, if they originate from *bad clusters*, you'll instantly feel resistance. *Don't fight those feelings!* They're expressions of one of your *protectors*. Welcome the feelings, embrace and invite them. Now ask yourself:

> ➤ *What color does this feeling have?*

Almost each time this question is asked, a color pops up. Don't ask yourself whether the color is right or not. Your subconscious is a sophisticated computer that works a million times faster than your conscious brain. It doesn't make mistakes! If the color that pops up isn't the final color you need, consider it as a gift from your subconscious as a necessary step to reach the final color. Just let go, let the river of your mental images flow wherever it wants. Once the color is known, ask it:

> ➤ *What shape do you have?*

Again, allow your subconscious to come up with whatever it wants. Let it happen spontaneously. Don't direct your thoughts. Allow your subconscious to unfold its full potential without direct rational interference.

Once you've consciously become aware of the color and shape, you've identified one of your *protectors*. Now, continue.

Invite this protector, this color and shape, into your safe place with your higher self.

Realize that regardless of what you might experience, feel or think about your *protector,* his intentions are always positive and caring. Therefore, always approach your *protectors* with love and respect. Your next question is:

> ➤ *What is it that you want?*

You will get direct answer. This might be something like: *I want to slow you down;* or: *I want to make you tired;* or: *I want to make you angry;* or: *I want you to feel disgust, etc.* Your first impulse might be that this has nothing to do with protection or care. Just continue on and be surprised.

> ➤ *Why are you doing this? What end result do you want to achieve? What exactly do you want to protect me from?*

Now your *protector* will reveal the purpose of its actions. The *protector* might say: *I want to make you feel tired/angry/disgusted so you'll stop pursuing what you're doing, because if you don't stop you will be hurt or get sick.* At this point you have to be aware of the fact that your *protector*'s carrying knowledge about an event in your past that you're consciously unaware of at this time. So, your *protector* totally reacts out of the feelings that were present during and right after the *bad cluster.* Your *protector* had no access to your total database in the same way that your conscious brain had no access to the small database of the *protector*. In a way, you could say they're both located on your hard-drive but in different partitions.

Your friend mechanism is blocking the subconscious from delivering the images of your protectors to your conscious brain because these are tied to *bad clusters*. But that's all going to change now. Explain to your *protector*:

> ➢ *At this point in my life, I need to get rid of feelings and beliefs that inhibit me from being happy and getting what I need and want. I respect the power you have and how you use it to protect me. Can you change your approach and belief systems and use your force to help both of us?*

Your *protectors* are a reflection of you, at a specific event, at a specific moment in your life. It's a little piece of your life that stored information when your mind was disconnected from your body, but it's still *your* mind! This memory was too disconnected from the normal pattern of your regular database, so it created its own little database of the event. Of course, all your protectors want to change for the better, they're one with you; they are you! Every positive transformation is in their interest as well as in yours. After the protector has agreed, repeat your last question:

> ➢ *How can we turn it around and use our powers to create positive energy?*

If *you* are unsure about how to change the inhibiting belief systems into positive ones, I can assure you, *your higher self* and your *protector* do know. Therefore your next step is:

> *Ask your higher self and your protectors how to transform your inhibiting belief system into positive, motivating ones.*

Once the first step of the belief system transformation is made, we'll go on to the next. The entire transformation will be completed when you've transformed the *source* of the old inhibiting belief. That source is the *bad cluster* that empowers the belief system. As long as the *bad cluster* hasn't been transformed, you'll keep on experiencing resistance whenever you try to apply a new positive belief. When the *bad cluster* has been transformed, you won't experience any resistance at all as you apply your new beliefs.

The *protector* or *your higher self* may instantly come up with new positive belief systems to replace the old ones, but they may also want to go to the content of the *bad cluster* first. Whatever they come up with, follow it. They're your guides in this process. You don't consciously know where to look for the *bad cluster*, but they do. You are hindered by your *friend mechanism*, but they aren't. Therefore, don't try to control the process, just follow their lead.

Whether your *protector* has already clarified how his inhibiting powers can be transformed into positive energy, or not, whether you've already agreed to new belief systems in every circumstance, or not, continue the same way by asking the *protector:*

> *How old was I when you started helping me?*

The age will instantly pop up. Once again, you're working in another level of awareness. Whatever pops up, go with that without reasoning or arguing.

When your *protector* was created, he escaped your physical body. Therefore, the following questions are not directed at the *protector*, although doing that might help you now and then. Ask yourself or *your higher self*:

> ➤ *Where am I? Am I somewhere outside or inside?*

Just go with any image that pops up and allow the connected feelings to come up. Regardless of what the first image is, that's the one you're looking for. If the answer is *inside*, you ask:

> ➤ *Am I in a small room or I in a big room?*

Once you've got the answer from *your higher self* transmitted directly by an image of a location or even just by a feeling, proceed by asking:

> ➤ *Is it cold or warm here?*

Once you know, ask:

> ➤ *Am I alone or are there others with me?*

What you are doing is making an *inventory* to provide you with a clear picture of the *what, when* and *where*. This enables you to be there at *that* moment in time and relive the event. This enables your brain to process the event, and analyze and store it with the correct emotional (*relative*)

codes, since it wasn't able to do this before.[13] Now that you know the *what, when* and *where*, the next step is to find out what caused your *protector* to arise and help you.

The following answers to your questions can come to mind very smoothly and without resistance. This is the most important moment of the transformation process. Maybe you'll feel some resistance here and there but just continue without hesitation. Don't rationally interfere with the process. Just wait for *spontaneous* answers in the shape of mental images. Take your time with the following questions and answers. Ask *your higher self* and the *protector* to guide you as soon as you feel resistance or if the process becomes stuck.

> ➢ *What's happening to me there?*

> ➢ *What is the most disturbing moment in that event?*

> ➢ *What is the most disturbing detail in that moment?*

Don't rationally interfere with the process. Just wait for spontaneous answers in the shape of mental images.

I can't repeat it enough times: Your rational brain will never be able to answer these questions. To find the most important *moment* and *detail* in the *event,* your rational brain is of no use. If it would be, you would have found the answers a long time ago. So, if it's not your rational thinking that'll provide the correct answers, what will?

---

13 For more details about the how and why, read Desirable Power.

ALLOWING *ALL* IMAGES

AND ACCEPTING *ALL* FEELINGS

Whenever you go from the _event_ to the _moment_, and from the moment to the _detail_, you'll experience your feelings intensifying. If you're feeling the physical and/or emotional symptoms intensifying, you know you've reached the next level (*event – moment – detail*). Once you've found that specific detail and your body is responding to it, you're basically doing nothing. You just stay focused on that detail and your feelings, until … spontaneously, a new picture pops up.

This new memory (mental image) is now your new _event_. Follow the same procedure as you did with the first event. Follow this formula repeatedly until the whole transformation of the *bad cluster* is completed.

Event – Moment – Detail – Feel – Spontaneous new image

Never underestimate *your higher self* or your *protector* in this process. Whatever mental image (picture, feeling, sound, smell, etc.) they offer you, go with that. They can't make mistakes in this process. The only one making a mistake would be *you* if you'd decide to back off at this moment. You're almost there, just go with the flow and experience the unbelievable relief and power that will be released when the entire content of the *bad*

> *Whatever mental image (picture, feeling, sound, smell, etc.) your subconscious offers you, go with that.*

cluster has been revealed. This process takes place literally, in seconds!

How do you know you've really transformed the *bad cluster*? Believe me, you will know, without any doubt! Seconds before the content of the *bad cluster* reveals itself, you will experience an escalation of your feelings. These feelings are not unknown to you, although in a lighter form, you've experienced them whenever the particular *bad cluster* had been activated in the past. The moment you fully become aware of its content, all the tension and whatever negative feelings are there in your body will disappear instantly, in seconds, forever. It will leave no doubt in your mind and body that you've transformed the negative power of the *bad cluster* into positive, healing and motivating energy.

> *The moment you fully become aware of its content, all the tension and whatever negative feelings are there in your body will disappear instantly, in seconds, forever.*

The very same moment that you've transformed the driving power behind your inhibiting belief systems, all the connected belief systems will lose their negative influence and your new empowering belief systems will be fully charged to guide and motivate you in whatever you wish to achieve.

It's imperative to realize that your brain is not a rigid machine. The subconscious operates at a tremendous speed and with great flexibility. You should not be rigid in this process either.

It's immensely important that you learn to *let go*. You have to realize that your strong urge to hold on to control means that you've already lost it and you're not in control anymore. (It might take a while to understand the full impact of this statement.) Many students have said to me: *"I want to let go but I don't know how! What's the best way to let go?"* There is a very simple rule for that.

> ***Letting go means:***
>
> ***Always choose the direction***
>
> ***that evokes your strongest resistance.***

Remember that the *PMA belief system transformation process* takes place on another level of awareness. Never be rigid. Allow *your higher self,* your *protectors* and your subconscious to take you wherever and whenever they want to go. You'll be surprised to discover how powerful this process is when you allow it to grow to its full potential. Now, let's go ahead and start the transformation process of your inhibiting belief systems and their hidden driving force, *bad clusters*.

Chapter 12 – Imagine Your Future as Real

Before we continue on to the main part of the exercise, here is one more interesting aspect to boost your drive towards prosperity. Our subconscious brain works holographically. As you know, our subconscious has to process about a million times more data then will ever reach the conscious brain, to be able to create our conscious awareness. The holographic images used in this subconscious process are not just "technical data." They're unbreakably connected to feelings. To be able to activate emotions you have to activate mental pictures first. *Drive, motivation, longing* for success, the *desire* of money and wealth are all emotions.

> *To be able to activate emotions you have to activate mental pictures first.*

Why can children become totally enthused about a new toy or about an upcoming visit to a Disney theme park? They feel this emotion because they *imagine* themselves having the toy or actually being in the theme park. Can't you feel the excitement of driving your friend's Ferrari, especially if you've never driven one before? You feel the excitement because you *imagine* yourself already driving.

Reasoning never causes motivating imagination. Rationalizations are just plain data without feelings. Imagination, on the other hand, is built from holographic images, *clusters*, memories. The data in these *clusters* have *relative codes* that create physiological changes in your body.

You'll experience these physiological changes as emotions, drives, motivations, or – in other words, feelings.

If you wish to create a life of prosperity you have to realize it won't automatically drop out of space. Some *rational reasoning* about wanting to become rich won't motivate or drive you enough to reach your goals. You need emotions and feelings, to experience that drive! How do you create motivating feelings? By realistic imagination! The difference between *rational reasoning* and *realistic imagination* is easy to understand.

How do you create motivating feelings? By realistic imagination!

Consider the following two scenarios. You're sitting in a lazy chair. You're not really thirsty but it wouldn't hurt if you had a beer. It's warm outside and a cold beer would make a nice refreshment. Would this reasoning motivate you enough to get you out of your lazy chair and get the beer?

What if you wouldn't just reason about having a beer but *imagined* you'd already had one. You can see the bottle and hear the sound when you pour the beer in a glass. You see the little bubbles and the foam on top. You imagine how the soft foam is touching your lips, you can feel the bubbles in your mouth and follow the cold beer going down your throat.

Would the second scenario motivate you enough to get you out of that lazy chair and get yourself that beer? I bet it would. Why does this second scenario motivate you more than the first one? Because you *realistically imagined* you're already enjoying the beer. In your mind you already have the beer.

This process of motivation isn't any different with money or wealth. You have to *imagine* your financial future in a realistic way, as if you already have it! By doing so, it becomes real to you. This won't just create a powerful drive to motivate you to action, it will also make you much more aware of every opportunity that presents itself. You wouldn't even notice these opportunities if you'd just *rationally reasoned* about your financial future. So, what do you have to do to make your future as real as possible?

> *You have to imagine your financial future in a realistic way, as if you already have it!*

You have to find out exactly what it is you want.

> ➢ What kind of house do you want?

> ➢ How much money do you want to make per year?

> ➢ How much money do you want to have in the bank?

> ➢ How much money do you want to invest and in what?

> ➢ What kind of clothes do you want to wear if money wouldn't be an issue?

> ➢ What kind of car do you want to drive?

> ➢ Where do you want to live?

These and many others aspects of your future have to be clear to you, down to the detail.

Let's use the house as an example. It's not enough to know you want a bigger or a nicer home. You have to imagine the house as if it's already there. Imagine the location, shape, size and color. How big will the living room be and how many bedrooms? How does the kitchen look and what about the bathrooms? Where do you want your future home to be? And what's the view like when you look out the window?

Each of the details you used is a detail that you've seen somewhere and liked a lot.

Once you've visualized the shape, colors and size of your home, start decorating and furnishing it in the same detailed way. Do the same thing with your income and the amount of money in your bank account. Don't just say: *"I want a lot of money."* Be precise. How much do you want to earn each month? Write down a number and do the same for the amount in the bank. Make it much more than you have now, but keep it realistic.

What happens in your brain when you create these detailed realistic images? Our imaginations are built from bits and pieces of previously stored comparison material, *clusters*. This doesn't mean that you've ever seen a house exactly as you just imagined. What you have done is built your dream house from parts of homes you saw before and that you liked. Maybe you've combined the color of one home with the front door of another and the roof of a third home. Each of the details you used is a detail that you've seen somewhere and liked a lot. How do we know? If you wouldn't have liked these details, you'd never have wanted them as a part of your future dream house, would you?

The fact that your future home is created out of details that gave you a good feeling in the past has a powerful effect on your physiology. You've activated all the details from previously stored *clusters* and all these details have very positive *relative codes* attached. Now you've combined all these positively charged details into one new *cluster* about your future home. This accumulates all the positive feelings into one powerful desire, exactly what will give you the drive to realize the achievement of your desired home.

Some people find it very empowering to create their own "wish board." It's like a piece of cardboard onto which you glue on pictures, drawings, and writings to represent the exact images of your future. You hang it in a visible place so you'll be able to see it every day. Every time you look at it, all kinds of positively charged comparison material become activated and empower your drive. Whatever you do, make your future as realistic as possible.

> *Whatever you do, make your future as realistic as possible.*

Research has shown that the majority of people don't know exactly what they want. That's why there are so many poor people in a world of abundance. Rich people know exactly what they want and when they want it, and they always find a

way to get it. You'll have no drive or direction if you don't have a clear picture of your end goal.

Assume you're on a boat in the middle of a lake. You know you want to reach the shore but you have no idea on which side of the lake the shore is located. You could paddle around for days without ever reaching the shore if you wouldn't make up your mind and come up with a specific goal, a specific part of the shore that you want to reach.

Now assume you're on the same boat and you've lost one of the paddles, but this time you know exactly where to go and why. Something very important, something you've desired for a very long time is waiting for you at that exact place. You're looking around and discovered this location. You focus on it and start moving the boat in that direction, although you only have that one paddle. Now let's assume that last paddle breaks. What are you going to do? You're still focused on the exact place you want to go and you try and move the boat in that direction rowing with your hands. If that doesn't work you jump overboard and swim towards your goal. After all, you know exactly where to go. There's no doubt in your mind you'll reach that place on the shore.

You must have no trace of doubt that you will possess that exact amount of money, car, house, etc. that you've created in your mind.

Do you feel the difference between the first and the second scenario? In that same way, you must have *no trace of doubt* that you *will* possess that exact amount of money, car, house, etc. that you've created in your mind. Knowing exactly what you want, and applying the *PMA technique* will unquestionably open up the doors for you to reach that shore.

Chapter 13 – Your Beliefs about Making Money

We receive all our external information through our five senses. What have you heard, seen, tasted, smelled, and felt this far about the subject of money? The sum of this is stored in ordinary *clusters* and *bad clusters* in your subconscious database, and has created every one of your existing beliefs about money and wealth.

It's not just about your *overt* beliefs, but even much more about your *hidden* belief systems about money and wealth. We tend to openly express a whole set of positive beliefs on how much we like money and wealth. Who in his right mind doesn't want to be rich, right? So, why would I even have *one* single negative belief system about being rich? You'd be surprised. What you're saying isn't always what you really believe and what really dictates your behavior.

> *Who in his right mind doesn't want to be rich, right? So, why would you even have one single negative belief system about being rich?*

To be able to find your real belief systems, start paying attention to *all* the moments when you have the opportunity to gain money. What has stopped you from creating, finding, and exploiting all of these moments? What do you feel when a sudden financial opportunity presents itself?

Sometimes, people have some difficulties in discovering or recognizing their own belief systems with regards to money. I've created the following statements to assist you in finding your own negative belief systems. Actually, I recommend using this tool even if you don't have any difficulty in finding them. Don't think too long about the answer, just assign yourself a number based on your feelings and be honest.

Whenever you discover a statement that gives you even a low level of comfort, don't continue on to the next statement. First find all the related belief systems that create that discomfort and write them down. To follow the steps you might want to turn to the outline in *Chapter 18*. You'll find summaries of all the steps of the transformation procedure.

Let's start with the statements. Whenever you encounter the slightest resistance against one of the statements (lower then a 10) start the transformation process.[14] Number 1 stands for maximum discomfort and/or resistance against the statement, number 10 means you have no resistance or discomfort at all.

My feelings towards having the right to achieve wealth.

1❑ 2❑ 3❑ 4❑ 5❑ 6❑ 7❑ 8❑ 9❑ 10❑

My level of importance in making, earning, or having money.

1❑ 2❑ 3❑ 4❑ 5❑ 6❑ 7❑ 8❑ 9❑ 10❑

My level of commitment in time and effort to becoming rich.

1❑ 2❑ 3❑ 4❑ 5❑ 6❑ 7❑ 8❑ 9❑ 10❑

---

[14] See Chapter 18: *"PMA transformation outline"*

My commitment to investing in learning about getting rich.

1☐ 2☐ 3☐ 4☐ 5☐ 6☐ 7☐ 8☐ 9☐ 10☐

My ability to invent and develop new concepts to making money.

1☐ 2☐ 3☐ 4☐ 5☐ 6☐ 7☐ 8☐ 9☐ 10☐

My faith in my abilities to make my dreams and ideas come true.

1☐ 2☐ 3☐ 4☐ 5☐ 6☐ 7☐ 8☐ 9☐ 10☐

My level of trust in that I'll make enough money if I start my own business.

1☐ 2☐ 3☐ 4☐ 5☐ 6☐ 7☐ 8☐ 9☐ 10☐

My ability to prolong successful approaches or businesses.

1☐ 2☐ 3☐ 4☐ 5☐ 6☐ 7☐ 8☐ 9☐ 10☐

My ability to take powerful action at all necessary levels when I see a business opportunity.

1☐ 2☐ 3☐ 4☐ 5☐ 6☐ 7☐ 8☐ 9☐ 10☐

My level of confidence in making a large amount of money.

1☐ 2☐ 3☐ 4☐ 5☐ 6☐ 7☐ 8☐ 9☐ 10☐

My level of confidence about the financial value of my knowledge and skills.

1❑ 2❑ 3❑ 4❑ 5❑ 6❑ 7❑ 8❑ 9❑ 10❑

The level of my ability to promote my skills and qualities.

1❑ 2❑ 3❑ 4❑ 5❑ 6❑ 7❑ 8❑ 9❑ 10❑

My level of comfort in asking people for the money they owe me.

1❑ 2❑ 3❑ 4❑ 5❑ 6❑ 7❑ 8❑ 9❑ 10❑

My level of comfort in charging people based on my knowledge and results instead of receiving hourly wages.

1❑ 2❑ 3❑ 4❑ 5❑ 6❑ 7❑ 8❑ 9❑ 10❑

My level of believing it's easy to make money.

1❑ 2❑ 3❑ 4❑ 5❑ 6❑ 7❑ 8❑ 9❑ 10❑

My ability to recognize financial opportunities.

1❑ 2❑ 3❑ 4❑ 5❑ 6❑ 7❑ 8❑ 9❑ 10❑

My level of having a perfectly clear picture of how I'll earn and/or make money.

1❑ 2❑ 3❑ 4❑ 5❑ 6❑ 7❑ 8❑ 9❑ 10❑

My ability to ask family, friends, and/or colleagues for advice and guidance.

1☐ 2☐ 3☐ 4☐ 5☐ 6☐ 7☐ 8☐ 9☐ 10☐

My ability to spend money on professionals for advice and guidance.

1☐ 2☐ 3☐ 4☐ 5☐ 6☐ 7☐ 8☐ 9☐ 10☐

My ability to see my personal unique qualities and value.

1☐ 2☐ 3☐ 4☐ 5☐ 6☐ 7☐ 8☐ 9☐ 10☐

My level of trust and faith about my own capacities and value when others try to discourage me.

1☐ 2☐ 3☐ 4☐ 5☐ 6☐ 7☐ 8☐ 9☐ 10☐

My ability to believe that I can be rich and very happy.

1☐ 2☐ 3☐ 4☐ 5☐ 6☐ 7☐ 8☐ 9☐ 10☐

My belief that there is an abundance of money to become rich.

1☐ 2☐ 3☐ 4☐ 5☐ 6☐ 7☐ 8☐ 9☐ 10☐

The level of my emotional abilities to receive money, gifts or attention.

1☐ 2☐ 3☐ 4☐ 5☐ 6☐ 7☐ 8☐ 9☐ 10☐

The number of times that I picture myself extremely wealthy.

1❑   2❑   3❑   4❑   5❑   6❑   7❑   8❑   9❑   10❑

Whenever you feel resistance or get stuck, ask *your higher self* and your *protectors* for help and guidance. They're always there for you and will never resist helping you. Remember: *You are not alone in this process!*

Whenever you give yourself a low number on a statement, turn to *Chapter 18* and find *The PMA belief system transformation process form.* Just follow the steps as described in this chapter as you get to a low-scoring statement.

Chapter 14 – Your Beliefs about Using Money

The subjects in *Chapters 13 to 16* are all related to each other. *Making, using, keeping,* and *enjoying money* are topics in the transformation process that interconnect. Each of the chapters might reveal issues that block you from getting rich. If you haven't made a lot of money yet, you'll still have belief systems about how to use the money you've already acquired, even if it's just a hundred dollars. Let's find out what your feelings are about the following statements.

My level of luck with money.

1❑ 2❑ 3❑ 4❑ 5❑ 6❑ 7❑ 8❑ 9❑ 10❑

My level of having a perfectly clear picture of how I'll use and/or enjoy money.

1❑ 2❑ 3❑ 4❑ 5❑ 6❑ 7❑ 8❑ 9❑ 10❑

My level of ability to manage money in the most successful way.

1❑ 2❑ 3❑ 4❑ 5❑ 6❑ 7❑ 8❑ 9❑ 10❑

My ability to solve financial and business problems.

1❑ 2❑ 3❑ 4❑ 5❑ 6❑ 7❑ 8❑ 9❑ 10❑

My level of confidence in creating my own financial guiding principles.

1❑ 2❑ 3❑ 4❑ 5❑ 6❑ 7❑ 8❑ 9❑ 10❑

My ability to take financial risks.

1❑ 2❑ 3❑ 4❑ 5❑ 6❑ 7❑ 8❑ 9❑ 10❑

My ability to learn from financial failures and avoid repeating the same mistakes.

1❑ 2❑ 3❑ 4❑ 5❑ 6❑ 7❑ 8❑ 9❑ 10❑

My ability to recognize profitable financial opportunities.

1❑ 2❑ 3❑ 4❑ 5❑ 6❑ 7❑ 8❑ 9❑ 10❑

My level of courage in taking financial risks to make money.

1❑ 2❑ 3❑ 4❑ 5❑ 6❑ 7❑ 8❑ 9❑ 10❑

My ability to overcome financial setbacks and losses.

1❑ 2❑ 3❑ 4❑ 5❑ 6❑ 7❑ 8❑ 9❑ 10❑

My ability to delegate work and responsibilities to people capable of making money for me.

1❑ 2❑ 3❑ 4❑ 5❑ 6❑ 7❑ 8❑ 9❑ 10❑

My level of confidence to deal and communicate with rich and powerful people in my business field.

1❑ 2❑ 3❑ 4❑ 5❑ 6❑ 7❑ 8❑ 9❑ 10❑

My ability to stay open-minded to new business input and ideas to make money.

1❑ 2❑ 3❑ 4❑ 5❑ 6❑ 7❑ 8❑ 9❑ 10❑

My ability to think big in financial and business matters.

1☐ 2☐ 3☐ 4☐ 5☐ 6☐ 7☐ 8☐ 9☐ 10☐

Whenever you give yourself a low number on a statement, turn to *Chapter 18* and find *The PMA belief system transformation process form.* Just follow the steps as described in this chapter with every low-scoring statement.

Chapter 15 – Your Beliefs about Keeping Money

As soon as you have a lot of money, all kinds of people will appear in your life trying to convince you that they know the best way to invest this money for you. Just ask them how much money they're making a year. If they earn less than you do, they're not the right person to work with. If you're still having doubts about their qualities, then ask *your higher self* for advice. Let's see if we can discover some of your inhibiting beliefs about keeping your money.

My level of belief that I deserve to be rich.

1☐   2☐   3☐   4☐   5☐   6☐   7☐   8☐   9☐   10☐

My abilities to control my finances wisely.

1☐   2☐   3☐   4☐   5☐   6☐   7☐   8☐   9☐   10☐

My level of self-control in not spending money on useless things.

1☐   2☐   3☐   4☐   5☐   6☐   7☐   8☐   9☐   10☐

My level of investments in making money work for me.

1☐   2☐   3☐   4☐   5☐   6☐   7☐   8☐   9☐   10☐

My ability to attract trustworthy people capable of making money.

1☐   2☐   3☐   4☐   5☐   6☐   7☐   8☐   9☐   10☐

My ability to invest money to achieve a maximum result.

1☐ 2☐ 3☐ 4☐ 5☐ 6☐ 7☐ 8☐ 9☐ 10☐

My ability to create a regular pattern of income.

1☐ 2☐ 3☐ 4☐ 5☐ 6☐ 7☐ 8☐ 9☐ 10☐

My ability to develop and apply long-term financial strategies.

1☐ 2☐ 3☐ 4☐ 5☐ 6☐ 7☐ 8☐ 9☐ 10☐

My level of feeling comfortable when I lose money.

1☐ 2☐ 3☐ 4☐ 5☐ 6☐ 7☐ 8☐ 9☐ 10☐

My level of comfort when I'm in debt (mortgage, suppliers, personal loans).

1☐ 2☐ 3☐ 4☐ 5☐ 6☐ 7☐ 8☐ 9☐ 10☐

My level of comfort in dealing with business competitors.

1☐ 2☐ 3☐ 4☐ 5☐ 6☐ 7☐ 8☐ 9☐ 10☐

My level of satisfaction about my present financial status.

1☐ 2☐ 3☐ 4☐ 5☐ 6☐ 7☐ 8☐ 9☐ 10☐

My ability to live without financial worries.

1☐ 2☐ 3☐ 4☐ 5☐ 6☐ 7☐ 8☐ 9☐ 10☐

Whenever you give yourself a low number on a statement, turn to *Chapter 18* and find *The PMA belief system transformation process form*. Just follow the steps as described in this chapter with every low-scoring statement.

Chapter 16 – Your Beliefs about Enjoying Money

The amount of money you own doesn't define your ability to enjoy it. As a child, you were able to enjoy even the smallest amounts of money, such as the times when your parents gave you a little money to buy some candy. Why? Because it provided you with the opportunity to buy something that you wanted and gave you joy, even if it was just a candy. If you want to become rich and stay rich, you have to master the art of *enjoying* money. Even if you only own a little amount at this time, you can still enjoy it. Breathing, eating and drinking are necessities; living an enjoyable life is an art. The level of your ability to enjoy money is inversely proportional to your level of motivation to become and stay rich. Let's examine your emotional response to the following statements.

My level of admiring and appreciating rich people.

1❑   2❑   3❑   4❑   5❑   6❑   7❑   8❑   9❑   10❑

The level of my desire to associate with rich people.

1❑   2❑   3❑   4❑   5❑   6❑   7❑   8❑   9❑   10❑

My level of enjoyment in associating with rich people.

1❑   2❑   3❑   4❑   5❑   6❑   7❑   8❑   9❑   10❑

My level of living without complaining about my financial status.

1❑   2❑   3❑   4❑   5❑   6❑   7❑   8❑   9❑   10❑

My balance between the time I use for making money and spending quality time with my loved ones.

1☐   2☐   3☐   4☐   5☐   6☐   7☐   8☐   9☐   10☐

My level of appreciation and joy about what I already possess.

1☐   2☐   3☐   4☐   5☐   6☐   7☐   8☐   9☐   10☐

My level of being able to focus on what I have instead of what I don't have.

1☐   2☐   3☐   4☐   5☐   6☐   7☐   8☐   9☐   10☐

My level of comfort and joy when I buy something for myself.

1☐   2☐   3☐   4☐   5☐   6☐   7☐   8☐   9☐   10☐

My level of comfort when I restrain myself from buying something that I want but don't need.

1☐   2☐   3☐   4☐   5☐   6☐   7☐   8☐   9☐   10☐

My ability not to be jealous when someone owns more than I do.

1☐   2☐   3☐   4☐   5☐   6☐   7☐   8☐   9☐   10☐

My level of comfort in having a lot of money.

1☐   2☐   3☐   4☐   5☐   6☐   7☐   8☐   9☐   10☐

The level of controlling myself in overspending.

1☐ 2☐ 3☐ 4☐ 5☐ 6☐ 7☐ 8☐ 9☐ 10☐

My level of comfort when I have a lack of money.

1☐ 2☐ 3☐ 4☐ 5☐ 6☐ 7☐ 8☐ 9☐ 10☐

My level of independence to create status with money, cars, houses, clothes, etc.

1☐ 2☐ 3☐ 4☐ 5☐ 6☐ 7☐ 8☐ 9☐ 10☐

My ability to share money and wealth with others.

1☐ 2☐ 3☐ 4☐ 5☐ 6☐ 7☐ 8☐ 9☐ 10☐

Whenever you give yourself a low number on a statement, turn to *Chapter 18* and find *The PMA belief system transformation process form.* Just follow the steps as described in this chapter with every low-scoring statement.

Chapter 17 – Be the Happy Millionaire

If you're an entrepreneur or you've just decided to become one, then applying the information in this book will jumpstart your business. It will bring out the best qualities in you and you'll be amazed about the abundance of hidden possibilities and potentials you really possess.

A lot of people have been wealthy for a long time but they've never mastered the art of seriously enjoying their possessions. Some of them have even abused their possessions in a desperate attempt to buy happiness, good relationships and health. Time and again, they become confused, disappointed, or depressed when they find out it doesn't work this way. They have a hard time realizing they *can* have all those things in abundance; they just cannot buy them with money.

Others are somewhere in the middle, between the beginners and the wealthy. They make a good income but, deep down, they know they could do a lot better. When applying the *PMA belief system transformation process,* they will discover what has been inhibiting them for so long in achieving that

> *Try it now, without procrastination! You now have all the tools. The only thing you have to do is apply them!*

next level of success. Somehow they do feel they have it in them but it isn't until the *PMA* program that they'll find their true potential. They weren't aware of their *higher self,* their *protectors,* and the powerful force of *bad clusters* before *PMA.*

So, what are you going to do with this information? Try it now, without procrastination! You now have all the tools. The only thing you have to do is apply them! You'll discover that not one single part of the process is difficult. On the contrary, you already know all these things deep inside. You just needed someone to wake you up. All you need to do now is make the decision to apply what you've learned.

Will this transformation process work for everyone? If you apply it, absolutely! There's not a single doubt. Those who've already used the *PMA technique* are on a continuing path of growth and development. They're regularly contacting the *PMA Institute* for more information. It's for that reason that we've created *The Millionaire Weekend Seminars* and *Personal Coaching Programs* with a *PMA* coach.

> *Try it now, without procrastination!*
>
> *You already know all these things deep inside.*

How can I be so certain that the technique works? Because the entire program is based on the most recent findings in biology, psychology, neurology, physiology, and quantum physics. *Progressive Mental Alignment*® is not just a theory. *PMA* is based on specific aspects of our human nature and genetic programs. These aspects and programs are the same for all of us.

Feel thankful for the wealth you will attain. Ask *your higher self* how to master the art of living an exciting, joyful life and how to use your money wisely. Accept your hidden powers for success and start growing towards your full potential. Dare to

free yourself from inhibiting belief systems that suppress your full potential. You're much too valuable. You now have all the tools to become and remain a happy millionaire.

Enjoy the unbreakable relationship with *your higher self* for the rest of your life. Experience all the wonderful results that have already occurred in the lives of so many people who've practiced the *PMA technique*. I look forward to hearing *your* success story.

Chapter 18 – PMA Transformation Outline

Whenever you get stuck in the process, regardless at what point, return to *your higher self* for help and guidance. The following outline shows the steps of the *PMA belief system transformation process,* as described in *Chapters 10 and 11.*

> ➢ Create your safe place.

> ➢ Get acquainted with *your higher self.*

> ➢ Create detailed images of every aspect of your future and imagine it's certain you are going to receive them.

> ➢ Determine your levels of comfort and address the issues[15] that you want to transform.

> ➢ Find the related belief systems by asking the following questions:

>> o Is the figure that I gave myself on this statement realistic?

>> o Why do I believe it's realistic?

>> o Why do I believe I am at this level of comfort?

>> o Is this the desirable level of where I want to be?

>> o What belief systems stop me from getting where I want to be?

---

[15] To discover your inhibiting belief systems, please refer to the statements in Chapters 13 to 16.

- o What personal belief system forms the basis of my answer to this particular statement?

- o Am I satisfied with my score?

- o Would I like to change this belief system?

- o If the answer is no, why not?

- o If the answer is yes, what's stopping me from making the necessary changes?

➢ Allow the level of discomfort to intensify and ask:

- o What color does this discomfort have?

- o What shape does it have?

➢ Invite the *protector* and *your higher self* over to your *safe place* and ask your *protector:*

- o What is it that you want?

- o Why are you doing this? What end-result do you want to achieve? What exactly do you want to protect me from?

- o Are you willing to change your belief systems and use your powers in a more positive and beneficial way?

- o How can you transform your belief systems into new ones that serve you well and use your power to create positive energy?

> How old was I when you started helping me?

From this point on, start asking yourself:

> Where am I?

> Am I somewhere outside or inside? If you need guidance, ask *your higher self.*

> Am I in a small space or in a big space?

> Is it cold or warm there?

> Am I alone or are there others with me?

> What's happening there to me?

> In what position am I?

> Am I sitting, lying down, or walking around?

> What is the most disturbing *moment* in that *event*?

> What is the most disturbing *detail* in that moment?

Event – Moment – Detail – Feel – Spontaneous new image

> The new image is your next *event*. Keep repeating the process: *Event – Moment – Detail – Feel – Spontaneous new image*, until an (unconsciously) unknown picture pops up that gives you a total feeling of relief and empowerment.

After you've discovered the content of the *bad cluster,* if you feel strong relief, then you've successfully completed the

process of transforming your inhibiting belief system into positive empowering energy.

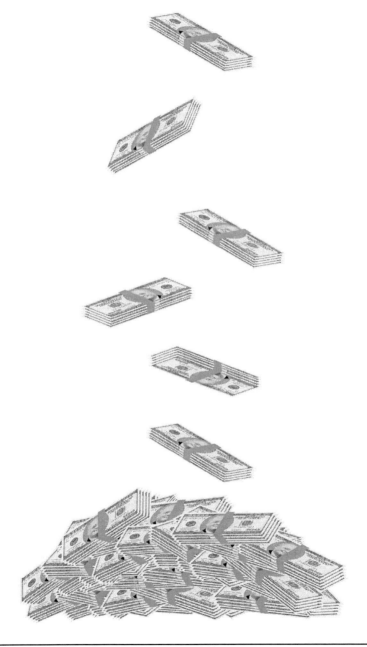

Desirable Power

Desirable Power is the accompanying textbook to the *Progressive Mental Alignment Technique.* It will show you how to control the hidden drives behind your belief systems, decisions, and behaviors. *PMA* has connected the scientific facts in psychology, neuroscience, physiology, quantum physics, and biology and discovered a new phenomenon called: *"Bad Clusters."* We all have *bad clusters.* They contain wrongly stored sensory data that carry a very powerful and negative physiological load. This physiological load controls at least 75% of all your belief patterns, and stores the root cause of all psychosomatic illnesses.

PMA is a scientifically underscored technique that locates and eliminates the destructive power of *bad clusters* and changes negative behavior into a proactive, energized, and healthy existence by freeing large amounts of concealed energy.

Desirable Power

Jacob Korthuis

Take control of your life,
health, career and relationships

Published in 2006
Author: Jacob Korthuis
ISBN: 0-9786598-1-3
ISBN EAN13: 978-0-9786598-1-3

Available in English and Dutch.

Desirable Power is available for $29.95 plus shipping and handling.

To order, please refer to our Online Shop at www.pmainstitute.com

The Personal PMA Coaching Session

A *personal PMA coaching session* is one of the most powerful ways to experience how you can discover deeply hidden sources of energy locked away in *bad clusters*, and how you can free their energy to achieve your desired goals.

In two-hour sessions, the *PMA coach* will assist you in locating and transforming the emotional blockers that prevent you from reaching your full potential. The focus will be on the specific areas in which you want to grow and remove the blockers that stand between you and success. This procedure is very direct and immediately effective.

Personal PMA coaching sessions are available for one-on-one sessions with a local *PMA coach*. Wouldn't it be great to experience this enlightening process without having to leave your home? Well, this is now possible. You can do a *personal PMA coaching session* with an experienced *PMA coach* while staying in your own living room, in your own comfy chair via a free Skype connection (internet).

Try a personal PMA coaching session from your own comfy chair via a free Skype connection (internet).

All you need is an internet connection, a web camera, and a headset and you'll be able to hear and see your *PMA coach* as if you're sitting face to face.

For more information contact us directly at info@pmainstitute.com or visit our website at www.pmainstitute.com

The Millionaire Weekend Seminar

The weekend seminar is an unforgettable event. It provides you with a deeper level of knowledge about *your higher self*, your *protectors, bad clusters* and shows you how to transform your inhibiting belief systems and the hidden source that empowers them.

The millionaire weekend seminar isn't just an amazing and intriguing program with lots of exercises; it's also your introduction to the unlimited potentials of the *PMA technique*. This seminar will form the basis for your own development in using *PMA* to transform your sabotaging belief systems and behavioral patterns into proactive positive energy.

PMA is a realistic and effective method for anyone who wants to achieve personal growth, get results, and take the findings of neuro-scientific research as a basis for action. Anyone who applies *PMA* correctly will achieve his desired growth. *PMA* has been thoroughly tested and is supported by the ultimate proof: it works. You're going to experience a level of freedom and creative energy that you never have before.

Feel free to contact us for more information and pricing at info@pmainstitute.com or visit our website at www.pmainstitute.com

The PMA Management Support Plan

Confronting the inhibiting feelings of employees and their emotionally charged conflicts is not only time consuming, it also drains the energy of many CEO's and their managers. Irritations, lack of motivation, and political power games have led to burnout amongst employees or corporate executives. Some managers are finding the solution by avoiding conflicts or trying to suppress emotions as soon as they present themselves. This, in fact, is an outdated model of addressing interpersonal activity. It used to be: *Emotions don't belong in the corporate world.* The *PMA technique,* is new, and looks at this differently. This technique specializes in implementing highly effective, successful solutions to conflict areas of human interaction.

The Management Support Plan is especially developed to remove the burden of daily tensions and complications from the shoulders of the CEO and the MT. This results in less stress, more available time, and improved productivity. The managerial and executive staff will now have more time and energy to focus on corporate growth and development in a well-balanced environment.

Learn more about:

❖ *The PMA creation program for core values and mission*

❖ *The PMA Inventory QuickScan*

❖ *The PMA Employment Procedure*

❖ *PMA Personal Business Coaching*

❖ *PMA Sales and Management Seminars*

The Management Support Plan is available as an extended ***program*** as well as a ***book***.

The **book** *The Management Support Plan* is available for $24.50 plus shipping and handling.

Published in 2008

Author: Jacob Korthuis

ISBN: 0-9786598-4-8

ISBN EAN13: 978-0-9786598-4-4

Available in English and Dutch.

To order, please refer to our Online Shop at www.pmainstitute.com

For information about the **program** please contact us directly at info@pmainstitute.com or visit our website at www.pmainstitute.com

The PMA Coach Education

The *PMA Coach Education* is conducted in two sessions of four consecutive days, from 9am to 9pm, along with an interval of three months to practice. The entire program is practice-directed. More and more coaches, trainers, and professionals in the field of psychology are adding the *PMA technique* to their existing approaches.

In addition to the explanations, much time will be spent on practicing the *PMA* tools. The working model of the *PMA method* will be set out based on the latest knowledge in the field of neuroscience, and in an easy way for anyone to understand.

Incorrectly encoded *bad clusters* aren't just the cause for all psychosomatic diseases; they're also the forces behind sabotaging behavioral and relationship problems. As soon as *bad clusters* are found and transformed, the positive energy that has so long been hidden, will form an unprecedented power source for healing and achieving full potential in every aspect of life.

Contact us for more information at info@pmainstitute.com or visit our website at www.pmainstitute.com